Perfect Phrases for
Sales and Marketing Copy

Also available from McGraw-Hill

Perfect Phrases for Sales and Marketing Copy

Hundreds of Ready-to-Use Phrases to Capture Your Customer's Attention and Increase Your Sales

Barry Callen

New York   Chicago   San Francisco   Lisbon
London   Madrid   Mexico City   Milan   New Delhi
San Juan   Seoul   Singapore   Sydney   Toronto

The McGraw·Hill Companies

Copyright © 2008 by The McGraw-Hill Companies, Inc. Printed in the United States of America. Except as permitted under the United States Copyright Act of 1976, no part of this publication may be reproduced or distributed in any form or by any means, or stored in a database or retrieval system, without the prior written permission of the publisher.

1 2 3 4 5 6 7 8 9 0 FGR/FGR 0 9 8 7

ISBN-13: 978-0-07-149590-5
MHID: 0-07-149590-8

This is a *CWL Publishing Enterprises Book* produced for McGraw-Hill by CWL Publishing Enterprises, Inc., Madison, Wisconsin, www.cwlpub.com.

McGraw-Hill books are available at special quantity discounts to use as premiums and sales promotions, or for use in corporate training programs. For more information, please write to the Director of Special Sales, Professional Publishing, McGraw-Hill, Two Penn Plaza, New York, NY 10121-2298. Or contact your local bookstore.

Contents

Contents

Contents

Contents

Contents

Contents

Preface

How to Use This Book to Find Your Perfect Phrases

The purpose of this book is to supply you with examples of phrases you can borrow or modify or use as guides to create your own communications.

In Chapter 1, you'll learn a few tips from the pros to improve the selling power of your writing.

It takes only a few minutes to read. Keep them in the back of your mind as you choose your phrases and modify them.

In Chapter 2, you'll find perfect phrases for the most important parts of your sales message, the parts common to almost every medium.

These are the parts that make or break your communication because they are what the recipients of your communication read most frequently. These include:

- Business and product names
- Slogans, theme lines, and taglines
- Headlines (your most important points)
- Subheads (your second-most important points)
- Calls to action (you ask them to do something)

In Chapter 3, you'll find perfect phrases for specific communication media.

Each advertising medium can do different things well. These phrases take advantage of those differences. These are the media covered:

Print Advertising

- Magazine and newspaper ads
- Brochures
- Posters and flyers
- Billboards
- Yellow Pages
- Classified ads

Broadcast Advertising

- Radio
- Television

Direct Mail

- Postcards
- Letters
- Sell sheets/product sheets/specification sheets
- Catalog product description
- Invitations
- Coupons
- Promotional offers

Web Sites

Press Release

There Are Two Ways to Use This Book

You can use this book to find perfect phrases according the advertising medium you are using. For example, you could choose to write a better direct mail piece or choose to write a better radio commercial. You simply go to the relevant section of Chapters 3 or 4.

You can also use this book to find perfect phrases for writing a piece of an ad common to all media, such as a headline. For example, you could be writing a better headline that will be used in a direct mail piece and a radio commercial. In that case, you should go to the Headline section of Chapter 2.

An Example of How to Use This Book to Write for a Specific Advertising Medium

Let's say you have a business teaching improvisational comedy to corporations, and you want to promote your business with an ad in a business journal.

Look up "Magazine and Newspaper Ads" in the table of contents, which you'll find in Chapter 3, Tactics for Print and Display Media.

A magazine ad consists of eight parts. Each part is created one step at a time and then the parts are combined in the final step.

Step 1. Select a photo or illustration.
Step 2. Create a headline.
Step 3. Create a subhead.
Step 4. Create a first paragraph.
Step 5. Create body copy.
Step 6. Create a call to action.
Step 7. Place your name or logo.
Step 8. Add your slogan.
Step 9. Assemble all the pieces.

In step 1, you're offered a choice of nine subjects for your photo or illustration:

- Your product or service
- A person using your product or service
- The benefit of your product or service
- The problem your product or service solves
- A satisfied customer
- A map showing your location
- A picture of your store or facility
- A dramatic demonstration of your product or service
- A cutaway view of the inside of your product

You choose to show a person using your service. So you select a photo of corporate employees enjoying your improv class as you teach.

In step 2, you go to the Headline section in Chapter 2. There, you are given a choice of 18 creative approaches to writing a headline:

1. State a tangible benefit involving time, money, safety, or ease.
2. State an emotional benefit that fulfills a desire or alleviates a fear.
3. State a problem and provide a solution.
4. Provide a demonstration.
5. Announce news.
6. Flag the prospect.
7. Ask a question.
8. Offer savings.
9. Offer freebies.
10. List helpful how-tos.

11. Tell a story.
12. Shock and surprise.
13. Use humor.
14. Use drama.
15. Use an expert endorsement.
16. Use a customer testimonial.
17. Work with an objection.
18. Associate with a good cause or organization.

You decide that the headlines under "State a problem and provide a solution" would work the best for your business situation.

There you can choose among five headline structures:

- Put an end to cockroach infestation with one phone call.
- Too many debts? Consolidate them and save.
- Need computer maintenance fast? Our team can be there in minutes.
- If you are losing customers, our loyalty programs can help.
- Dirty chimneys cleaned cheap.

You decide that putting an end to low morale is one of your customers' biggest problems. So you choose "Put an end to cockroach infestation with one phone call" as your model. You change it to "Put an end to low morale with one improv comedy class."

You use the same process for steps 3 through 8. Pick an approach you like, pick a phrase as a model, and then adjust the phrase to fit your particular business situation.

PHOTO:	CORPROV TEACHER AND CORPORATE EMPLOYEES ENJOYING AN IMPROV CLASS
HEADLINE:	Put an end to low morale with one improv comedy class.

SUBHEAD:	These games are so easy, even vice-presidents can do them.
FIRST PARAGRAPH:	If your idea of improving morale is a slide lecture pep talk on casual Friday, have we got a better alternative for you.
BODY COPY:	Our four-hour onsite improv comedy class is not only lots of fun, it can also improve your employees' teamwork, listening skills, creativity, ability to think on their feet, and presentation confidence.
CALL TO ACTION:	For more information, contact Barry Callen at 608.347.8396 or barry.callen@gmail.com.
LOGO/NAME:	CORPROV
SLOGAN:	Improv comedy classes for corporations.

An Example of How to Use This Book to Write a Headline Shared by Various Media

Let's say you have a catering business and you want to write a powerful headline to use in several media: a newspaper ad, a magazine ad, a postcard, and a flyer. You go to Chapter 2, under "Headlines," and you can choose among 18 creative approaches to writing a headline (as listed in the preceding example):

1. State a tangible benefit involving time, money, safety, or ease.
2. State an emotional benefit that fulfills a desire or alleviates a fear.

3. State a problem and provide a solution.

   …

You decide that the headlines under "State a problem and provide a solution" would work the best for your situation.

There you can choose among five headline structures.

- Put an end to cockroach infestation with one phone call.
- Too many debts? Consolidate them and save.
- Need computer maintenance fast? Our team can be there in minutes.
- If you are losing customers, our loyalty programs can help.
- Dirty chimneys cleaned cheap.

You decide that speed is one of your catering company's strengths. So you take the headline "Need computer mainte-nance fast? Our team can be there in minutes."

Then you make that headline your own. Here are three examples of how you might do that:

- Need catering fast? Our team can be there in three hours.
- Need catering fast? We can deliver a complete banquet for 40 by this time tomorrow.
- Need a catering estimate fast? We can have one ready for you within the hour.

It's as easy as that. Just find the perfect phrases that best fit your message and medium and use them to create your perfect communication.

For more examples of ads and marketing communication using the principles in this book visit **www.barrycallen.com**.

Acknowledgments

This book is the result of 30 years in marketing communications. So I'd like to thank God for keeping me alive—through lightning strikes and bungie jumping accidents—long enough to achieve my life's dream of writing a book.

Thanks first to John Woods of CWL Publishing Enterprises, who asked me to write this book and worked with me in its development and to his ace editor Robert Magnan, who carefully went through the manuscript. I also want to acknowledge Donya Dickerson, the editor at McGraw-Hill who came up with the idea for this book and had faith in me to write it—thanks Donya. And thanks to author David Wright and to Linda Gorchels of the University of Wisconsin Graduate School of Business, who gave me my first teaching job and referred me to John.

Thanks to my family for their patience with my writing schedule: Patti, Paige, and Lexie Callen. Thanks to my Mom and Dad for encouraging my love of reading and writing.

Thanks to all the folks who gave an unknown, untried guy his dream job as a copywriter on the Shell Oil Account at Ogilvy & Mather in Houston: Gail Faget, Jo Lynn Rogers, Patti Kurtz, Donna Price, Barbara Sher, Richard Bolles, David Ogilvy, Robert Caples, Pat Daugherty, Bill Pemble, Jim Mohr, Paul Norris, Bob Marberry, and Joe Kilgore. You changed my life and gave me a kick-ass career.

Thanks to all my colleagues, clients, and mentors for sharing your wisdom and investing several hundred million dollars on my creative ideas. Thanks to Betty Marquardt, Kay Plantes, J'amy Owens, Judy Faulkner, Katie O'Brien, Jody Glynn Patrick, Joan Gillman, Mickey Brazeal, Lorene Moothart, Dave Chew, Liz Carroll, Holly French, Jennifer Bennerotte, Donna Fletcher, Jane Brotman, and Jane Biondi. Thanks to the brain trust at The Hiebing Group, a truly market-led communications company, for giving me the creative helm and for encouraging process R&D. Specifically: Roman Hiebing, Marion Michaels, Scott Cooper, Mike Kelly, Dick Kallstrom, Steve Krumrei, Emily Child, Chris Schell, Mike Pratzel, Nancy Kobus, Barbara Hernandez, David Florin, Sean Mullen, David Schiff, Carl Fritscher, Jeane Kropp, Jacqi Fleissner, and Sandy Geier.

Thanks to all my teachers, friends, and fellow students at The Hoffman Institute, Second City Improvisational Theater, "Without Annette" Improv Comedy Group, the Madison Contact Improv Dance Group, and the Re-evaluation Co-counseling group. You made me a better teacher, moderator, thinker, speaker, and therefore, writer.

Thanks to the friends who love me, including: Nell, Betty, Kimberly, Kay, Brian, Al, Tom, Dena, Carmen, Sharon, Joey, Martha, Joy, Jude, Dave, David, Holin, Annette, and Liz.

And thank you, gentle reader, for buying this book. May it help you make big bucks.

Perfect Phrases for Sales and Marketing Copy

Chapter 1
Basic Principles for Writing Better Sales and Marketing Copy

Eight Principles for More Effective Communication

As you choose and modify the phrases you want to use, there are some principles to keep in mind that will make your sales and marketing copy far more effective.

Look Through Your Customers' Eyes, Not Your Own

You know more about your business and care more about your product or service than your customers ever will. Their reasons for buying your product are probably very different from your reasons for selling it. So as you write, err on the side of simplification and avoid professional jargon.

Don't assume your customers know why a particular feature is important or valuable to them. Explain the benefits to them.

Even if you are talking to expert specialists, it pays to write more clearly and simply.

Most professional advertising writers aim for a fifth- or sixth-grade reading level, because most readers aren't really paying attention.

Follow the Path of Least Resistance

It takes a lot of time and money to try to change people's minds. You are far better off building on their current perceptions. Find a way to reinforce something they already believe and tie that belief directly to buying your product.

If you find yourself talking about what people should do, you are preaching, not marketing. The power of marketing lies in accepting the way people are. Seek the smallest possible change in their behavior that is required to get them to buy your product or service.

Don't Be Logical, Be Psychological

People are both rational and emotional. But it is emotion that drives attitude and behavior. For example, it is not rational to overeat and become dangerously obese, but people do. The reasons people give for buying things (e.g., "A Mercedes is a well-made car and therefore a good investment") and their real reasons (e.g., "A Mercedes shows my high income and higher social status") are two different things.

Behavior is the result of fear and desire. When the desire exceeds the fear, people act. Your goal in writing sales and marketing copy is to increase desire and reduce fear.

In general, our emotions beat up our intellect and take its lunch money. So make sure you choose the most emotional, powerful words you can get away with using. For example, "bulletproof" is more emotionally powerful than "safe."

Organize Information Around a Single Power Idea or Theme

Our lives have become so complex and information has become so abundant that consumers can handle only one main idea per communication. They simply won't devote the energy to prioritizing lists of features. They expect you to find the main point or theme and stick with it. If the main point interests them, they will read on. If not, they won't.

Your headline, your name, your tagline, and your opening paragraph are all places to state your main point. Readers read these first. A good rule of writing sales and marketing copy is "When in doubt, leave it out."

Be Conversational: Write to Express, Not to Impress

A sign stating that "It is highly recommended that male members of the species should ambulate in the direction of their left extremity to seek a place in which to relieve themselves" is not nearly as effective as "Men's Restroom: Turn Left." Be conversational in your writing. Write like you speak. To check your style and vocabulary, read out loud what you write.

Shorter Is Better

The average reader will give you a half second or less to determine whether or not to pay attention to your communication. So, shorter is better.

Use shorter words. Write shorter sentences. Break up long paragraphs into short ones. Break up long documents into short paragraphs. Use bullets. Use phrases. Be brief.

Most people no longer read. They scan.

Concrete, Specific, and Visual Language Is Always Better

Use words you can draw a picture of. You can't draw a picture of a "solution." But you can draw a picture of a "consultant." Abstract words like "quality" are bad. Concrete words like "golden" are good.

Our minds are visual. Good writing conjures up concrete, specific, visual images.

Don't Brag About It—Prove It

There's a big difference to people between bragging and proving. Bragging is words. Proving is facts.

This is bragging: "Our company is the recognized leader that offers the highest-quality products and the friendliest service." This is proving: "98% of our customers return every year. When surveyed, 60% of our customers would recommend our products to their friends because of durability and 30% because of friendly service."

People no longer trust their government, their religious leaders, and even their news media. Why should they trust a business they don't know that is trying to sell them something?

Chapter 2
Fundamental Components
of Effective Sales and
Marketing Copy

A ll communications are not created equal. There are certain words and phrases you have to get right because they are what the recipients of your communication read first and most often. These most critical, highest-impact words and phrases include:

- Business and product names
- Slogans, theme lines, and taglines
- Headlines (your most important points)
- Subheads (your second most important points)
- Calls to action (you ask them to do something)

These words and phrases tend to occur within almost every marketing communication.

Business and Product or Service Names: Who Are You?

Your single most important word and phrase is your *name*. Your name is the one word or phrase that appears in every communication about you.

Some researchers believe that a good business name can enable you to charge up to 20% more for the same goods and services.

Think of your name as a bucket into which you pour all your communications. If your name is forgettable, unclear, or just plain wrong, it is as if that bucket has holes and your marketing dollars are leaking out, wasted.

The majority of the words in the English language are currently owned by someone. So you have to find ways to make the words you choose ownable. You can do this by inventing a new word, a new combination of words, a soundalike, or a new spelling. You should have a lawyer do a legal search on your name to make sure it is available, ownable.

There are some proven approaches to naming that can make your name more memorable, relevant, attention-getting, and likeable. For example, people tend to like names that conjure up concrete visual images (Hillside Insurance) over names that don't (First Amalgamated Insurance Corporation). And people prefer names that are easy to say and spell (The Golden Group) over those that are not (The Aerodynamiconic Enterprise Institute).

23 Creative Approaches to Naming a Business, a Product, or a Service

1. COMBINATION

Take two words (from your business area or from your consumer benefits) and combine them.

- Taxpro Accounting
- Foodbreak Restaurants
- Weldrite Fabricators

2. SOUNDALIKE

Spell your name phonetically, to represent the sound of the name.

- Klipt Hair Salon
- Soffwhere Programming
- Art-kitecture

3. PHRASE

State your name as a phrase that a customer might say.

- Cute Shoes
- I'm Ready for My Close-up Children's Photography
- I Need to Rent a New Tool

4. BENEFIT

Identify your chief customer benefit and build it into your name.

- Compumatch Dating Service
- Speedy Remodeling
- Likemom's Restaurant

5. VISUAL IMAGE

Create a concrete visual picture by using an object as your name.

- Gavel Legal Services
- Paintbrush Graphic Design
- Gardenia Gift Shop

6. OXYMORON

Pair two opposing characteristics.

- Stronglite Welding
- Freshtorn Blue Jeans
- Richpour Molasses

7. ALLITERATION

Join two or more words that begin with the same letter or sound.

- Capital Cabinets
- Eddy's Eatery
- Ready Rentals

8. RHYME

Create a two-word name that forms a rhyme or similarity of sound.

- The Finer Diner
- Sweet Treats Bakery
- The Ancient Merchant (antiques)

9. FOREIGN

To evoke sophistication or fun, borrow a word from another language or culture.

- Parthenon Builders

- Oui Café
- Mañana Bed and Breakfast

10. PLACE

To provide stability and legitimacy, select a place that evokes appropriate associations.

- Niagara Home Water Systems
- Sahara Dehumidifiers
- Prairie Software Design

11. WORDPLAY

For a sense of fun or friendliness, play on words.

- Hair Studio 54
- Nice Buns Bakery
- Pros & Concrete

12. MYTHOLOGY

Identify a god, a goddess, a mythical creature, or a fictional character famous for the characteristics you wish to associate with your name.

- Sherlock Diagnostics
- Phoenix Remodeling
- Zeus Electrical Contracting

13. ANIMALS

Identify an animal, an insect, or a plant known for the characteristics you wish to associate with your name.

- Fox Modeling Agency
- Rhino Industrial Equipment
- Dragonfly Delivery Service

14. COLORS

Make your name more vivid and memorable by giving it a color.

- Orange Optical Shop
- Viridian Landscaping
- BlueSky Consulting

15. PERSONAL NAMES

Find a real person to personify your business in a relevant way.

- Mbutu's Imports
- Rembrandt Housepainting
- Jones/O'Hallaron Investments

16. LETTERS

Use letters and/or numbers rather than words.

- H.A.H.A. Comedy Club
- I-8 Roadside Diner
- W.G.F. (We Grow Profits)

17. UNRELATED BORROWING

Borrow a word from an unrelated area and combine it with a word relevant to your business.

- Mr. Furniture
- Snaptastic Photography
- 101 Donations

18. SOUND EFFECT

Think of a sound that represents how someone feels or what happens when your product or service is used.

- Flush Plumbing
- Holy Cow! Ice Cream Shop
- Whoosh Delivery Service

19. VERBS

Create a sense of action by selecting a relevant verb.

- Harden Concrete
- Blossom Nursery
- Zap Pest Control

20. PERSONIFICATION

Invent a character to personify your brand.

- Grandma Anna's Toy Shop
- Two Roofers and a Ladder
- Aunt Leah's Frozen Custard

21. TARGET MARKET

Make your customers part of your name.

- Homeowners Interior Design
- Visitors' Guide to Duluth
- Moms Deserve Chocolates

22. SLANG

Use a common phrase to make your name catchy and memorable.

- Honest-to-Goodness Car Repair
- Far Out Computer Games
- Stone-Cold Ice Delivery

23. CATEGORY LABEL

Literally describe your product or service or your business category.

- The Plumber's Plumber
- The Tooth Doctor
- Kilnfire Ceramics

Slogans, Theme Lines, and Taglines: What's Your Hook?

How is your business different? Why should your customer be interested in you?

A slogan, theme line, or tagline is the summary that signs off your communication. It usually follows or precedes your business name. On a Web site, it should be right there at the top, to quickly let people know what you can do for them.

A good tagline should answer one or more of three key questions:

1. What do you do?
2. For whom do you do it? Whom do you serve?
3. How are you different from other companies with similar products or services? What makes you best?

Readers of your advertising are unlikely to go digging for the answers to these three key questions. Put the answer(s) in your tagline, so they can quickly determine if your ad is relevant. If it is, then they will spend more time with your ad.

Most advertising taglines are too generic. For example, "People helping people with technology" could be used for many different businesses.

Don't be afraid to be literal and descriptive, especially if you are in a new, little-known, or little-understood business or technology category. This is imperative if your name does not indicate what you do. For example, "Acme Corporation. Computer Recycling."

All the rules that apply to selecting or creating a name apply to a tagline. The more concrete, visual, emotional, unusual, specific, and easy to say, the better.

There is no rule that says your brand has to have a tagline. But generally, you are better off having one.

23 Creative Approaches to Writing a Tagline, a Theme Line, or a Slogan

1. ASK A QUESTION

Instead of making a specific promise, ask a question the consumer would like to hear or to ask.

- Why not do it right the first time?
- What does your suit say about you?
- Where else can you get it all done at once?
- Why not you? Why not now?
- Which way do you want to live?
- How can you stay on top of the latest trends?

2. USE ALLITERATION

Repeat the first letter of at least two words in your tagline.

- Better bids for bigger bucks.
- Concrete quality counts.
- Intelligent. Informed. Insightful.

3. USE RHYME

Rhyme at least two words in your line.

- All of the caring, none of the swearing.
- Unleash your inner winner.
- Flexible textable messaging.

4. USE RHYTHM

Create a rhythm by repeating sounds or by using two words with the same number of syllables. For example, one-syllable words like "Frat Rat," two-syllable words like "Entrance Inside," or three-syllable words like "Merrily Verily."

- We're movers, not shakers. (moving company)

- We know when to leverage what you know.
- Bridal. Floral. For all.
- Bric-a-brac.

5. USE AN OXYMORON

Create two opposing thoughts or include two words with opposite meanings.

- Cool fireplaces.
- It's stupid not to use the smartest technology.
- Because the only constant is change.

6. TIE IT TO A NAME

Put your name in the tagline. This works particularly well when your name is a word in English or will be recognized as a word.

- Czsimaligentri Realty. Hard to pronounce. Easy to work with.
- Bernard Kutz cuts hair.
- Susan Golden Investments. When you're with us, you're golden.

7. POSITION WITH ASSOCIATIONS

Work with ideas that people have of your business area. Be proud to be different. This approach is particularly good if your category is disliked or distrusted. Convince customers that you are not like the stereotypes associated with your business area.

- Not your garden variety nursery.
- Our lawyers are no joke.
- Just like mother used to make—but without the guilt.
- Forget everything you know about car mechanics.
- Where the old rules no longer apply.

- Consulting, reinvented.
- Like no roofers you've ever seen.
- We're where doctors go when they get sick.

8. POSITION AGAINST COMPETITORS

Claim that you are better than or at least different from your competitors.

- The area's only 24-hour emergency service.
- Where the customer is queen.
- They say it. We do it.
- No one has more experience with ASP systems.
- The industry's number-one supplier.
- The first is still the best.
- When you can't afford a mistake.

9. KEEP IT SHORT AND CONVERSATIONAL

Borrow a simple phrase or word that most people say or recognize.

- We'll take it from here.
- Need some help?
- Just around the corner.
- Night and day.

10. USE AN ANALOGY, A SIMILE OR METAPHOR, OR A SYMBOL

Find something everyone knows that is like your brand, feature, or benefit.

- The top of the mountain.
- Always have a safety net.
- As loyal as an old friend.
- Like a solid foundation.

11. PAINT A PICTURE

Describe a situation, tell a story, or find a symbol that is concrete, specific, and visual.

- Modaff's Used Cars. We take the high road to fair prices.
- Veronshky's Deli. A cut above grocery store meat.
- Anglon's Advertising. Target marketing for bull's-eye profits.

12. DRAMATIZE IT

Dramatize or exaggerate the problem, the benefit, or how the customer will feel about it.

- Make sure you end up with more money than retirement years.
- If it was any more fun, it would be illegal.
- Don't wait until your car breaks down.

13. TIE IT TO A PHYSICAL ATTRIBUTE

Select a physical characteristic of your product that you can own, like color, shape, size, smell, taste, sound, or motion.

- The purple wine in the spiral bottle.
- The little speaker with the big sound.
- Look for the man in the sparkling white van.

14. INCLUDE YOUR CUSTOMERS

Identify the type of individual or group of people who are most likely to use your product or service—or exclude people who are unlikely to use it.

- For parents who care about their children's education.
- The I.T. department for businesses without I.T. departments.
- Honk if you love antique cars.

- Revolution Paintball: For the warrior within.
- Don't get our music? Then get out.

15. TIE IT TO A TIME OR A PLACE

Own the occasion or location or situation or time when people are most likely to need or use your product or service.

- Weddings and only weddings.
- It's time you took a family vacation.
- Montana range-fed beef.
- Visit Switzerland in America.

16. EXPRESS A FEELING

Either describe the feeling or state the feeling as if quoting one of your customers.

- Yippee!
- I've never done that before.
- Check it off the list.

17. STATE A POSITION

Express something that you think or believe that will resonate with members of your target market.

- Where single moms get equal pay.
- Anything worth doing is worth doing well.
- There's a lot more to life than business meetings.

18. CALL FOR ACTION

State what you want your customer to do with your product or service or how, when, or where they will use it.

- Eat it up.
- Come back for more.
- Send a friend a flower.

- Take it to the bank.

19. STATE A BENEFIT

Identify the end result, the aim or goal, or the ultimate way in which your product is beneficial.

- Gifts that get noticed.
- Get more done in less time.
- Put an end to household pests.
- The non-jargon get-it-done-today-so-you-don't-have-to-worry-about-it computer repair service.
- Feel the freedom!

20. USE UNUSUAL WORDS

Borrow words from other languages or slang. Make up words. Organize your words in unusual ways, such as a poem or a telegraph message.

- There once was an inn in Nantucket.
- Ery-vay un-fay ids-kay oys-tay!
- Rivers. Mountains. Forests. You.
- Bonjour!
- Doggamit! Dog-training for difficult dogs.

21. MAKE IT THE VOICE OF A CHARACTER

Say what a spokesperson, a diligent employee, or a customer might say.

- It's not just my job, it's my calling.
- Everybody in the pool!
- Cheap, fast, or good? Pick three.
- My, my, my, but that's tasty.

22. PLAY WITH WORDS

Create a memorable and relevant tagline by playing on your business name or your business category. It also conveys a sense of fun.

- We rub you the right way. (massage therapy)
- Accounting that measures up.
- Surveying that's on the level.
- Burritos bigger than your boca.
- A cut above the rest. (hair salon)
- Housecleaning with Kindness (proprietor: Arlene Kindness).
- We take care of your overhead. (roofers)

23. USE YOUR CATEGORY DESCRIPTOR

If your name does not identify your business category or if your prospects are unfamiliar with your business category, then strongly consider using your category descriptor as your tagline.

- Emergency furnace and air-conditioning repair.
- Robotic manufacturing process software design.
- Homemade pies for restaurants, delivered fresh daily.
- Women's health clinic.

Headline: What's Your Most Important Point?

A headline is the most important phrase you can use to get attention or interest. Your headline should make your single most important point, whether in print or on radio or television.

Your headline should be so compelling it will arrest the readers' attention, so that they decide to check out the rest of your ad.

The best headlines are both relevant and unexpected. They fit the situation and yet they stand out from other ads. Since around 80% of readers will read only your headline, it is important that you make it count.

Here are some proven types of headline approaches.

Use these proven creative approaches below to write headlines for your business or product.

18 Creative Approaches to Writing a Headline

1. STATE A TANGIBLE BENEFIT INVOLVING TIME, MONEY, SAFETY, OR EASE

- Our college graduates earn 20% more.
- Reduce your chances of burglary and theft.
- New tool requires less muscle effort.
- Become pain-free in under an hour.
- Increase annual productivity per employee.

2. STATE AN EMOTIONAL BENEFIT THAT FULFILLS A DESIRE OR ALLEVIATES A FEAR

- Feel 10 years younger.
- Never worry about sewage problems again.
- Give your family a vacation memory they'll always treasure.
- Make your money work harder so you can relax.
- Find the career of your dreams online.

3. STATE A PROBLEM AND PROVIDE A SOLUTION

- Put an end to cockroach infestation with one phone call.
- Too many debts? Consolidate them and save.
- Need computer maintenance fast? Our team can be there in minutes.
- If you are losing customers, our loyalty programs can help.
- Dirty chimneys cleaned cheap.

4. PROVIDE A DEMONSTRATION

- Even at 120 below zero, this car battery starts right up.
- Which one is the drawing and which one is the photograph?
- This console is so simple to use, even a three-year-old can master it.

- Crumpling up this page will make more noise than this fan.

5. ANNOUNCE NEWS

- The (company name) Grand Opening Celebration is this weekend.
- Expanded summer hours beginning June 1.
- Introducing a brand new way to keep your lawn maintained.
- (Employee name) is now a member of the (company name) family.
- Our Back to School Sale starts early this year.
- Cold winter predicted. Get your car winterized before it's too late.
- Our new patented inspection technology can reduce waste up to 33%.
- Announcing a breakthrough in business consulting software.

6. FLAG THE PROSPECT

- Thinking about getting divorced? Call our lawyers first.
- Introducing a health clinic for women, by women.
- If you like chocolate, you'll love our new store.
- Attention, migraine sufferers. Get instant relief.
- Seniors get an automatic 20% discount.
- Serving the men and women in our armed forces since 1942.
- If you think an applet is a small apple, don't visit our Web site. (insider technical jargon)
- Bed-Stuy B-Boys B breakin' it down here Saturday night. (insider slang)
- ¡El dinero no compra el amor! (foreign language)

7. ASK A QUESTION

Use the five W's—who, what, when, where, and why—to provoke your reader.

- Who says you can't take it with you?
- What can you do right now to increase your return on investments?
- When is the right time to buy a house?
- Where can you go to find a great chiropractor?
- Why do we triple-reinforce our truck shocks?
- How can we offer you twice as much for half the usual price?
- Which type of manager are you?
- Are you sure you have enough insurance for your family to live on?

8. OFFER SAVINGS

Contact your lawyer before advertising a promotional offer.

- Buy one, get one free.
- Save up to 50% with this coupon.
- Announcing our Back to School Sale.
- $100 off if you purchase before Sept. 1.
- Why chase sales when you can enjoy our low prices every day?
- The lowest price—or we'll refund the difference.
- For a limited time, we're cutting prices as much as 10%.

9. OFFER FREEBIES

Contact your lawyer before advertising a free offer.

- Get a free safety inspection with every oil change.
- Buy one, get the second half-price.
- The first 50 callers also get a free T-shirt.

- Clowns, prizes, rides, and free balloons for the children.
- Two free lottery tickets with every purchase over $50.
- Sign up for our rewards program and get preferred customer benefits.

10. LIST HELPFUL HOW-TOS

- Ten ways to reduce your income taxes this year.
- How to increase your returns and lower your investment in equipment.
- Five things you should know to order wine for a client.
- This year's 20 best gifts for teenagers.
- What to do when your customer won't pay you.

11. TELL A STORY

- How one old man accidentally invented the fishing lure that revolutionized an industry.
- When Dr. Smith is not doing surgery here in town, he's volunteering to help the poor in Calcutta.
- Recognize this ten-year-old gymnastics student? He grew up to be an Olympic gold medalist.
- The plumber and the diamond ring.
- How we turn the world's best beef into the world's tastiest sandwich.
- Ever wonder what goes on inside your furnace?

12. SHOCK AND SURPRISE

- You may have cancer and not even know it!
- The average kitchen cutting board wouldn't pass a restaurant food inspection.
- Surprise! You have been selected for a free home inspection.

- If a disgruntled employee walked in with a gun, would you know what to do?
- Ten things your accountant will never tell you unless you ask.
- One year from now, 5 out of 10 new businesses will be out of business.

13. USE HUMOR

- If you don't have a good accountant, may we suggest a good lawyer?
- Our printing quality is a lot better than this newspaper ad.
- You didn't start your business to become a secretary, janitor, and bookkeeper. But we did.
- Is your supplier's idea of a cost estimate to add a zero and multiply by two?
- Optometrists with vision.

14. USE DRAMA

Try to think of a situation where the stakes are higher than average.

- It's 3:15 AM. Your factory line just shut down. You're losing $1,589 per minute. How soon can you get a replacement part?
- 15 minutes after the tornado flattened our house, our agent was there with food and water.
- Without the carbon monoxide detector, the Smith family would have died on Christmas Eve.

15. USE AN EXPERT ENDORSEMENT

- All our mechanics are ASE-certified as Master Auto Technicians.

- "Dr. Smith got me back in the game." Jamal Johnson, Super Bowl-winning quarterback
- As seen on television.
- Named the city's number-one employment contractor by In-Town Magazine.
- Rated among America's ten best veterinary clinics by the National Board of Veterinary Science.

16. USE A CUSTOMER TESTIMONIAL

Look for extreme customer behavior or for individuals with great credibility.

- "We drive over 100 miles just to get our hair cut there." Willa and Bob Smith
- "I don't just trust my children to any day care provider." Heather O'Malley, mother
- Why Carl Virona has been coming to our restaurant every Friday night for 23 years.
- "They have integrity." Reverend Malcolm Washington, First Baptist Church

17. WORK WITH AN OBJECTION

Acknowledge a typical bias, opinion, or problem in the headline and then refute it in the body copy.

- Not all mechanics are out to rip you off.
- The problem with lawyers is that they are all sharks. Right?
- Most advertising doesn't work. Ours does—and we can prove it.
- An expert is someone who knows more than you do. So how do you know if you can trust them?
- Introducing a radical idea: computer technicians who speak plain English.

18. ASSOCIATE WITH A GOOD CAUSE OR ORGANIZATION

- For every dollar you spend on purchases this December, we'll donate a portion to Orphans Without Toys.
- P.T.A. members can save 20% on book purchases at this event.
- Show us your A.A.R.P. membership and get an instant 10% off all prescription drugs.

Subheads: What Point Comes Second?

Your subhead goes directly under or after your headline. Think of it as a second headline that makes your second most important point. It should amplify the meaning of your headline and provide a natural transition to the rest of your communication.

Make sure that recipients of your communication get your subhead second, not first. In printed materials, you can do this by placing the subhead below the headline or by using smaller type than for the headline. In radio or television, you can do this by placing the headline first in the script and the subhead second.

Avoid duplicating the point in the headline. The easiest way to do this is to use a different creative approach.

For example, if your headline states a problem, you can use the subhead to state the solution.

Headline: Need computer maintenance fast?

Subhead: Our team can be there in minutes.

But a good rule of thumb is to use two different types of phrases, as in the example below.

Headline: Has it been 20 years since you went on a first date? ("Flag the prospect.")

Subhead: Look and feel that much younger after a day at our spa. ("State an emotional benefit that fulfills a desire or alleviates a fear.")

You can mix and match types of headlines and subheads as you see fit.

Call to Action: What Do You Want Them to Do?

Ask your customers to take action now. This action could be a change in attitude, a change in behavior, or a search for additional information. You could ask them to call, stop by, order now, request information, contact you, or take advantage of a promotional offer. It is not always necessary to ask customers to buy your product. Sometimes that request is implied automatically.

Three Creative Approaches to Writing a Call to Action

1. ENCOURAGE PROSPECTS TO ACT NOW TO AVOID LOSING SOMETHING

- Order now while supplies last.
- Hurry, offer ends June 23.
- A preventive checkup now could save your life.
- The longer you wait to repair your roof, the costlier the damage.
- Don't miss this once-in-a-lifetime event.
- Find out if you're paying too much for health insurance.

2. ENCOURAGE PROSPECTS TO ACT NOW TO GAIN SOMETHING

- The sooner you order, the sooner you can enjoy your new swimming pool.
- Order now and receive a second bag of salt absolutely free.
- The 100th caller today will receive $1000.
- Be the first one in your neighborhood with a giant plasma screen TV.
- This weekend only, save up to 50% on all brand-name merchandise.

3. ENCOURAGE PROSPECTS TO TAKE SMALL, LOW-RISK STEPS

- Visit our Web site at www.barrycallen.com.
- For more information, call Barry Callen at 608.347.8396.
- Order today and receive a free one-month trial absolutely free.
- Call now to schedule a free personal insurance review.

- Stop by our store Monday through Sunday 9 AM to 9 PM and see our wide selection for yourself.
- To receive your free booklet on how improv can improve your next corporate retreat, contact Barry Callen at 608.347.8396 or barry.callen@gmail.com or visit www.barrycallen.com.

Chapter 3
Tactics for Print
and Display Media

Magazine and Newspaper Ads

Most ads printed in newspapers or magazines consist of eight parts. Except for the main visual and the logo, all the parts are words and phrases.

1. Main visual
2. Headline
3. Subhead
4. First paragraph
5. Body copy
6. Call to action
7. Logo or name
8. Slogan

But readers no longer read. They scan. As a result, some parts of your print ad are more important than others: the main visual, the headline, and the logo or name are the first items readers look at. Your readers will look at them and know in under a half second whether they will read the rest of the ad. So pay extra attention to making these elements dominant, relevant, and unexpected.

If readers decide to pay attention to your ad, they will next look at the subhead (second-priority headline) and the first paragraph and then the call to action. Only then will they actually read the remaining paragraphs (body copy).

> **Time-Saving Tip:** You can use almost the exact same material for both your print ads and your brochure: same visuals, same headline, etc. Not only will this save you time, it will also help reinforce your message and make it more memorable. Professionals believe this repetition ("integrated marketing communications") helps build "brand equity" for a higher long-term return on your communications investment. Make sure all your communications are singing the same tune.

Dos and Don'ts

- Do use graphic design to create a hierarchy of dominance to guide the readers' eyes from the most important thing, to the second-most, to the third-most, and so forth.

- Don't make the readers work hard or think too much to find what is important on the page.

- Do use powerful selling words, like *free, new, now, introducing*, and *save*.

- Do avoid general and abstract words like *quality, convenience, advanced, partnership*, and *solutions*.

- Don't reverse out the type in your body copy (white letters on a black background). It can reduce readability as much as 60%.

- Do make one main point per ad—and then prove it.

- Don't make your ad a long list of different claims.
- Do make sure you include a call to action. It can increase results as much as 20%.
- Don't imitate what your competitors are doing. Do stand out.

Nine Steps to Creating a Print Ad

To create your print ad, create the eight parts and then put them all together.

Step 1. Select a photo or illustration.

Here are some classic subjects for your photo or illustration:

- Your product or service
- A person using your product or service
- The benefit of your product or service
- The problem your product or service solves
- A satisfied customer
- A map showing your location
- A picture of your store or facility
- A dramatic demonstration of your product or service
- A cutaway view of the inside of your product

Step 2. Create a headline.

The headline should state your single most important point. (Use the creative approaches presented in Chapter 2, pages 21–27.)

Step 3. Create a subhead.

The subhead should state your second-most important point. Make sure the headline and subhead don't duplicate each other. Use type size and placement to make sure the recipients read the headline first and the subhead second. (Use the creative approaches presented in Chapter 2, page 28.)

Step 4. Create a first paragraph.

Think of your first paragraph as a third headline. It should make your third-most important point. It should flow naturally out of your headline and your subhead and hook the recipients enough to pull them into the body copy.

Your first paragraph should also function as the beginning of the body copy, to be followed by the middle and the end of the body copy. The middle amplifies or proves the point you are making in the first paragraph. The end is a call to action.

The key in writing the first paragraph is to continue coming up with new selling arguments. One way to do this is to continue using a different type of headline to inspire the opening paragraph. Don't duplicate what you have already said. You can again refer to the list of types of headlines (pages 21–27) for inspiration or you can use the ideas shown on pages 37–42 to get started.

Step 5. Create body copy.

This is where you provide more detail and proof for those readers who are interested.

At this point, you have readers hooked and potentially interested in your sales proposition. Now you must overcome their inner skeptic with reasons to believe. These are largely concrete details that prove your claim is true. You may want to do a second paragraph, or a third, or more, depending on how much you need to explain. The best rule of thumb is that less is more. Avoid duplicating earlier points. See examples on pages 43–44.

Step 6. Create a call to action.

At this point you have gotten the attention of the reader with your headline, subhead, and opening paragraph and you have amplified your message in the middle paragraph. Now you are ready to close the sale in the final paragraph. You are going to ask your readers to take an action. This action could be a change in attitude, a change in behavior, or a search for additional information. You could ask the readers to call, stop by, order now, request information, contact you, or take advantage of a promotional offer. (Use the creative approaches for writing a call to action in Chapter 2, pages 30–31.)

Step 7. Put your name or logo.

In general, you should place your logo in the lower right of your ad or in the bottom at the center. (For a better name, use the creative tips in Chapter 2, pages 7–11.)

Step 8. Add your slogan.

Your slogan should generally run either just below your logo or at the bottom of your ad. (For a better slogan, use the creative approaches in Chapter 2, pages 13–19.)

Step 9. Assemble all the pieces.

Use type size, boldness, and placement to establish a clear hierarchy of dominance: a most important thing, a second-most important thing, and so on. This will help guide the readers' eyes to the most important things in your ad. Be sure to leave a lot of white space. Break up large blocks of words into smaller blocks.

11 Creative Approaches to Writing a First Paragraph of a Print Ad

1. STATE THE MOST IMPORTANT THING YOUR COMPANY, PRODUCT, OR SERVICE WILL DO FOR CUSTOMERS

- Our college graduates earn 20% more.
- Fix a flat without a jack or a lug wrench.
- Avoid costly legal fees.
- Reduce your transportation costs up to 15% through better scheduling.
- Keep your frozen foods from melting in a power outage.
- To sell more, convert more prospects.
- Titanium-lattice microfibers add strength.
- Won't bend, chip, or splinter.

2. STATE WHY CUSTOMERS SHOULD CARE ABOUT THE POINT YOU MAKE IN THE HEADLINE AND SUBHEAD

- If you like everything in its place, you'll love our office organizing system.
- Can't afford to lose your key employees?
- Could you use a little R&R after that big M&A?
- Your professional reputation means everything.
- Fix the repairs that nag at you every day.

3. STATE WHOM YOUR COMPANY SERVES, WHAT YOU DO, AND HOW YOU ARE DIFFERENT

- Our financial planning firm is far more dedicated to preserving your hard-earned capital than commission-based investment firms.

- We don't just make trucks to sell to everyone. We make trucks that can save a firefighter's life.
- Our publishing company specializes in serving K–12 educators, so we make our textbooks affordable and approvable.
- We stand for one thing: safety. All our scuba gear is designed for safety first.
- We're not like most corporate law firms. If we can keep you out of court, we will.
- We understand the needs of the handicapped, because we only hire the handicapped.
- We eat, drink, and sleep electronic control systems.

4. OPEN WITH A SURPRISING FACT

- Chances are your restaurant kitchen counter has more bacteria than a dog's mouth.
- By the time you read this, your competitor may already have called us.
- The number-one cause of plane crashes is not human error. It's human hair.
- It's hard to believe, but studies show that you're better off without some customers.
- Your greatest financial loss is not caused by the market, the economy, or your customers. It's caused by your divorce.
- Firms in Third-World countries are flooding the market with chalk disguised as essential lifesaving prescription drugs. How do you know if you bought some?
- If health care costs continue to rise, we'll all be working for a hospital by 2026.

5. OPEN WITH A PROMOTIONAL OFFER

Consult your lawyer before advertising a promotional offer.

- Get $10 off if you stop by on any Tuesday before 5 PM.
- Announcing our New Year's Day Gift Exchange Sale.
- Buy three, get one free. That's the deal.
- To celebrate our grand opening, we're offering the first 50 couples free admission.
- In honor of George Washington's birthday, we're taking $1 off every purchase.
- Get a free makeover with every makeup purchase over $20.
- Save up to 30% on your first purchase with this coupon.
- If you love shoes, you'll love the perks that come with our Preferred Shoppers card.
- Come in today. We'll match the lowest price in town.

6. CHALLENGE ONE OF THE CUSTOMERS' ASSUMPTIONS

- Are you really sure you have enough insurance protection?
- The secret to Six Sigma quality is not pushing your employees harder.
- Contrary to popular belief, chocolate doesn't cause zits.
- You have a greater chance of losing a customer to poor service than to a lower price.
- Surprise. Nobody expects an industrial accident.
- If you think that all you have to do is build a better mousetrap, may we sell you some Florida swampland?
- You don't become a millionaire just by working harder. You also have to work smarter.

- Can you spot the flaw in this picture that will result in a lawsuit? We can.
- Believe it or not, your next new business opportunity is right under your nose.

7. OPEN WITH NEWS

- Thanks to the new tax code, you can now deduct more of your capital gains.
- This week's weather forecast calls for six inches of snow. It's time to winterize your engine.
- A big New York bank just bought your local bank. Think everything will remain the same?
- The Acme Company wins top honors at the international software society.
- We'd like to welcome our newest associate, Bob Smith. Bob brings 10 years of experience ….
- Introducing a milkshake so thick you can drink it upside down.

8. STATE WHY YOUR TOPIC IS TIMELY. ANSWER THE QUESTION, "WHY NOW?"

- With interest rates at record lows, there's never been a better time to buy a mortgage.
- Beat the Christmas rush and order your gifts online today.
- It's cold and flu season. How warm is your winter coat?
- If you don't get your order in early, you may have to wait up to a month.
- When you're waist-deep in water, it's too late to wonder if you have flood coverage.
- Hurry! Supplies are limited. Offer is good only while supplies last.

- Be the first to have a 3-D television in your neighborhood.

9. SHOW YOU UNDERSTAND THE CUSTOMERS' POINT OF VIEW BY DESCRIBING IT

- You hate waiting in line. So do we. So we added more cash registers.
- It's 3:00 a.m. Your child has a fever of 102. Should you call the doctor?
- If you think most savings and loans are the same, you're right. But we're different.
- We understand what it's like to lose $1,000 a minute when your line breaks down.
- Sometimes it seems like no one wants to do business with you if you're not rich.
- If your idea of a good time is beer, BBQ ribs, a big-screen TV, and a sudden-death overtime, have we got a sports bar for you.

10. ACKNOWLEDGE A DIFFICULT TRUTH AND THEN STATE WHY CUSTOMERS NEED NOT WORRY ABOUT IT

- The fact is, you can't trust most car mechanics. Fortunately, ours have to pass the test of integrity.
- Just because you don't have enough money doesn't mean you shouldn't get great service.
- Yes, our custom windows cost up to 10% more. But they last 100% longer.
- If you're not absolutely satisfied, we'll give you a full refund, no questions asked.
- We all die sometime. But our cardiac center can help you live a long, full, active life.

- Are you used to less than perfect housecleaning? We only hire perfectionists.

11. SUMMARIZE YOUR MAIN PERSUASIVE ARGUMENTS

- There are three reasons to choose us as your distributor: only 1% administrative costs, global reach, and real-time status reporting.
- In a nutshell, our people are so experienced that they make fewer mistakes, which saves us money and enables us to charge you less.
- We started creating product displays over 20 years ago in a tiny garage in Edmonton, Alberta. Today, we have over 3,000 locations worldwide.
- We are the world's safest airline. Now we'd like to prove it.

Four Creative Approaches to Writing Body Copy for a Print Ad

1. LIST MULTIPLE FEATURES, SERVICES, AND/OR BENEFITS

- Our in-house marketing communication services include marketing strategy, media strategy and buying, new media, graphic design, advertising, public relations, and broadcast and print production.

- We have over 30 service locations around the world, including the United States, Canada, Mexico, Brazil, China, South Korea, Japan, New Zealand, Hong Kong, Singapore, and all members of the European Community.

- There are multiple advantages to using a centralized data repository for all your individual patient records. Changes are made instantly. Different departments can better integrate care. Doctors can be alerted to potentially adverse drug reactions. More efficient real-time billing can improve cash flow. The net result is better patient care for less money.

2. PROVIDE REASONS TO BELIEVE YOUR MAIN CLAIM

- Our client list includes 50 of the country's Fortune 500 companies.

- Over 40% of all insurance customers are processed by our back-room operations with less than a .00001% error rate.

- Nine out of ten brides say they would recommend our catering service to their best friend.

3. GIVE AN EXAMPLE

The best examples are mini-stories involving people in problem situations who were helped by your product or service. The more vivid, detailed, and dramatic, the better.

- In the North Sea last October, the power went out on a 20-person rig. The rig was at least two hours from the nearest helicopter rescue station. As temperatures plunged below zero, our safety room enabled all 20 men to survive with no loss of life and no need for medical care.

- While on a business trip over 2,000 miles from home, Susan hit a telephone pole while traveling 65 miles an hour. Her rental car was totaled. Fortunately, the air bag worked and she walked away without a scratch. The local rental agent had a car waiting for her within one hour. He delivered it to the hospital himself.

- According to Robert X, the VP of Information Systems at X, Inc., that one system redesign suggestion saved his company over $100,000 last year in returned merchandise.

4. USE PHOTOS/ILLUSTRATIONS AND CAPTIONS

- (beautiful color photo of bridal bouquets) Caption: All our bouquets are fresh-cut that day.

- (photo of industry award) Caption: Our company has received the international industry award for most innovative design for three of the last five years.

- (cutaway diagram showing the inner workings of a machine) Caption: Note the absence of complex gears and belts. This reduces downtime and simplifies maintenance.

Brochures

Most printed brochures consist of nine parts. Except for the visuals, the logo, and the indicia, all the parts are words and phrases. Since people tend to scan rather than read, some parts of your brochure are more important than others.

The outside front panel is the *most critical*, followed by the outside back panel. Recipients will look here first to determine whether or not your brochure is worth paying attention to.

On these outer panels, the most important information is the main visual, the headline, the tagline, and the logo or name. Your recipients will look at them and know in under a half second whether they will devote attention to the rest of the ad. So pay extra attention to making these elements dominant, relevant, and unexpected. If your brochure will primarily be on display in a rack, make sure the important information will still be visible on the upper half of your front panel.

Once readers decide to pay attention to your ad, they will next look at the subhead (second-most important thing), the first paragraph (third-most important thing), and then the call to action (what you want them to do). Only then will they actually read the remaining paragraphs (body copy).

> **Time-Saving Tip:** As mentioned earlier, you can use basically the same visuals, same headline, etc. for your brochure as for your print ads. This will save you time and help reinforce your message, make it more memorable, and build "brand equity." While you communicate the same core message in both mediums, you may want to provide more explanation in the brochure. People generally expect brochures to be more detailed and informative.

Dos and Don'ts

- Do put extra attention on your front and back panels. These are the most highly read.

- Do use graphic design to create a hierarchy of dominance to guide the readers' eyes from the most important thing, to the second-most, to the third-most, and so forth.

- Don't make the reader work hard or think too much to find what is important on the page.

- Do leave plenty of white space to make your layout more inviting.

- Do use powerful selling words, like *free*, *new*, *now*, *introducing*, and *save*.

- Do avoid general and abstract words like *quality*, *convenience*, *advanced*, *partnership*, and *solutions*.

- Do use color to add recognition, vibrancy, and highlights to your brochure.

- Don't reverse out the type in your body copy (white letters on a black background). It can reduce readability as much as 60 percent.

- Do break your words into easy-to-read chunks or lists. Number your points or use bullets.

- Don't make your brochure a long list of claims. Have a single dominant theme and then use the details to prove that theme.

- Don't clutter your layout with multiple logos, multiple slogans, multiple locations, multiple phone numbers, etc. This makes you look cheap and disorganized.

- Do have as much white space as filled space in your brochure, as a general rule of thumb.

- Do put fine print and legal copy somewhere out of the way where it doesn't interfere with the basic content.

- Do make sure you include a call to action. It can increase results as much as 20 percent.
- Don't imitate what your competitors are doing. Do stand out.
- If you plan to mail your brochure, do check your finished layout with the Postal Service to make sure it meets mailing standards.

TIP: How long should your brochure be?

Brochures can come in many formats and lengths. Generally, they are printed in four-page increments, so your choices are four pages, eight pages, 12 pages, and so on. The most common brochures are a single 8 ½- by 11-inch or 8 ½- by 14-inch sheet of paper printed on two sides and folded into three or four panels.

In general, the length of your words should be determined by the number of compelling new selling arguments. Don't repeat yourself within a brochure. It should also be determined by your intent. If your customers are not expecting to receive your brochure and it is intended to interrupt their attention, make the brochure shorter. If customers request more information, you can make the brochure longer.

Ten Steps to Creating a Brochure

To create your brochure, create the nine pieces of your brochure and then put them all together.

Step 1. Select a photo or illustration.

Here are some classic subjects for your photo or illustration:

- Your product or service
- A person using your product or service
- The benefit of your product or service
- The problem your product or service solves

- A satisfied customer
- A map showing your location
- A picture of your store or facility
- A dramatic demonstration of your product or service
- A cutaway view of the inside of your product

Step 2. Create a headline.

The headline should state your single most important point.

In a brochure, you get the opportunity to put different headlines in three important places: on the front panel, on the back panel, and on the inside panel. To make sure your headlines are not too similar, use different creative approaches for each headline. (Use the creative approaches presented in Chapter 2, pages 21–27.)

Step 3. Create a subhead.

The subhead should state your second-most important point. Make sure the headline and subhead don't duplicate each other. Use type size and placement to make sure the headline is read first and the subhead is read second.

In a brochure, as you have the opportunity to use three different headlines, you also can use three different subheads on the front panel, on the back panel, and on the inside panel. To make sure your subheads are not too similar, use different creative approaches for each subhead. (Use the creative approaches presented in Chapter 2, page 28.)

Step 4. Create a first paragraph.

Your first paragraph should work as a third headline: it should make your third-most important point. It should flow naturally out of your headline and your subhead and pull the readers into the body copy.

Your first paragraph should also function as the beginning of the body copy, to be followed by the middle, which amplifies or proves the point you are making in the first paragraph, and the end of the body copy, which is a call to action.

The key in writing the first paragraph is coming up with new selling arguments. One way to do this is to continue using a different type of headline to inspire the opening paragraph. Don't duplicate what you have already said. You can again refer to the list of types of headlines for inspiration or you can use the list on pages 52–57.

Step 5. Create body copy.

This is where you provide more detail and proof for those readers who are interested.

At this point, you have readers hooked and potentially interested in your sales proposition. Now you must overcome their inner skeptic with reasons to believe. These are largely concrete details that prove your claim is true. You may want to do a second paragraph, or a third, or more, depending on how much you need to explain. The best rule of thumb is that less is more. Avoid duplicating earlier points. See pages 58–60 for examples.

Step 6. Create a call to action.

You have gotten the attention of the reader with your headline, subhead, and opening paragraph and you have amplified your message in the middle paragraph. Now you are ready to close the sale in the final paragraph. You are going to ask your readers to take an action. This action could be a change in attitude, a change in behavior, or a search for additional information. You could ask the readers to call, stop by, order now, request information, contact you, or take advantage of a promotional offer. (Use the creative approaches for writing a call to action in Chapter 2, pages 30–31.)

Step 7. Place your name or logo.

In general, you should place your logo at the very top of the front panel, on the left top side of the rear mailing panel, or at the bottom right of the inside panel. (For a better name, use the creative tips in Chapter 2, pages 7–11.)

Step 8. Add your slogan.

Your slogan should generally run either just above or below your logo. (For a better slogan, use the creative approaches in Chapter 2, pages 13–19.)

Step 9 (for self-mailing brochure). Add indicia.

If you decide that your brochure should be self-mailing, then there are some special things you will have to do. You will need indicia and you will need to devote the entire back panel of the brochure to mailing information.

An indicia is a rectangle that contains postal information (usually a special number or bar code) necessary to send your brochures through the mail at a bulk rate (usually a standard rate or third-class rate). To qualify for this special rate, your pieces must be identical, and you generally need to mail at least 500 at a time. You need to get your indicia from the Postal Service. The Postal Service is very particular about how the indicia and mailing panel should be laid out on the page and also particular about what information they should contain. They are also very particular about the size, shape, uniformity, and weight of your mailer.

Make sure you get your final brochure layout and information approved by your local Postal Service office before you get your brochures printed. If there's an error, you may need to order a second printing to correct it.

Step 10. Assemble all the pieces.

Use type size, boldness, and placement to make sure there is a clear hierarchy of dominance: a first-most important thing, a second-most important thing, and so on. This will help guide the readers' eyes to the most important things in your ad. Be sure to leave a lot of white space. Break up large blocks of words into smaller blocks.

11 Creative Approaches to Writing a First Paragraph for a Brochure

1. STATE THE MOST IMPORTANT THING YOUR COMPANY, PRODUCT, OR SERVICE WILL DO FOR CUSTOMERS

- Our cosmetics salespeople earn 18% more.
- Fix a leak without a weld or a pipe wrench.
- Avoid costly repair fees.
- Reduce your advertising costs up to 40% through a better media-buying strategy.
- Keep your security systems from shutting down in a lightning storm.
- To increase profits, identify and remove unprofitable customers.
- Natural herbal ingredients promote healing and reduce negative reactions.
- We won't leave you holding the bag.

2. STATE WHY CUSTOMERS SHOULD CARE ABOUT THE POINT YOU MAKE IN THE HEADLINE AND SUBHEAD

- If you like self-cleaning appliances, you'll love our new range.
- Can't afford to lose sales to your competitors?
- Could you use a larger R&D budget and smaller expectations?
- Your attention to detail affects everything your clients think about you.
- Fix the personnel problems that are behind the issues you face every day.

3. STATE WHOM YOUR COMPANY SERVES, WHAT YOU DO, AND HOW YOU ARE DIFFERENT

- Our retirement planning system is more conservative than Wall Street and more profitable than banks.

- We don't just make cameras to sell to tourists. We make cameras for journalists who can change the world.

- Our consulting firm specializes in billing and collecting, so we design our systems to prevent collection problems.

- We stand for one thing: freedom. All our vacation getaways let you choose how to spend your time.

- We're not like most savings and loans. We don't wait until it's sunny to loan you an umbrella.

- We understand the needs of the nonprofit world, because we serve only nonprofits.

- We have devoted our lives to the eradication of poverty worldwide.

4. OPEN WITH A SURPRISING FACT

- Chances are your computer system is vulnerable to a hacker in more than 10 ways.

- For every client complaint you hear about, there are 10 that you should hear about.

- Recruiting salespeople with optimistic explanatory styles can increase sales 80%!

- It's hard to believe, but cutting the number of products can actually boost profits.

- Your greatest business threat may well be your own health.

- Someone in China just purchased your product so they can learn how to make it and sell it for 50% less. What can you do about it?

- If you can't afford to guarantee your service, you can't afford to stay in business.

5. OPEN WITH A PROMOTIONAL OFFER

Consult your lawyer before advertising a promotional offer.

- Women get $10 off their first drink on Ladies' Night.
- Announcing our No Reason At All Super Sale.
- Buy two, get the third one free.
- To celebrate our grand opening, we've invited a celebrity to our party.
- In honor of finishing your taxes, we're offering 40% off every purchase.
- Get a free tire rotation with every purchase of two new tires.
- Save up to 10% on your next purchase with this rebate.
- If you love chocolate, you'll love the gift program for our preferred shoppers.
- Show us a competitor's receipt with a lower price and we'll match it.

6. CHALLENGE ONE OF THE CUSTOMERS' ASSUMPTIONS

- Are you really sure you have enough computing power?
- The secret to high morale is not paying your employees bigger bonuses.
- Contrary to popular belief, marriage does not cause divorce.
- You have a greater chance of dying in a car accident than on an airplane.
- Surprise. You weren't expecting a stroke.
- Nine times out of ten, it is better to be the first than the best.

- Making a million dollars won't make you a millionaire. Keeping the money will.
- Can you spot the electrical risk most likely to cause a fire? We can.
- Believe it or not, your true love may be a mouse click away.

7. OPEN WITH NEWS

- Thanks to the new real estate laws, you can now place your returns in an investment trust.
- This week's market forecast calls for a severe drop. It's time to switch to bonds.
- We're the proud new owners of your pet grooming service. Rest assured we'll continue to care for your pet.
- The Acme Company wins a lifetime achievement award.
- We'd like to welcome our newest affiliate, Des Moines, to our broadcasting family.
- Introducing a laptop so durable you can let your kid use it.

8. STATE WHY YOUR TOPIC IS TIMELY. ANSWER THE QUESTION, "WHY NOW?"

- With gold at record highs, there's never been a better time to buy master artworks.
- Beat the back-to-school rush and order your school supplies for next year.
- It's tax season. How much of your health care costs can you deduct?
- If you don't get your order in early, you may have to wait up to a month.
- When your assembly line has been stopped for one hour, it's too late to wonder if you skimped on lubricant.

- Hurry, supplies are limited. Offer is good only while supplies last.
- Be the first to offer your clients electronic access to worldwide distribution.

9. SHOW YOU UNDERSTAND THE CUSTOMERS' POINT OF VIEW BY DESCRIBING IT

- You hate being put on hold. So we make sure you talk to a person within 15 seconds.
- It's Christmas Eve. Only one toy can satisfy your child. Who should you call?
- If you think most box manufacturers are the same, you're right. But we're different.
- We understand what it's like to let employees go during a business downturn.
- Sometimes it seems like no one wants to help the little guy anymore.
- If your idea of a consultant is an expert from out of town with a box of slides who knows why everything can't be done, are you in for a pleasant surprise!

10. ACKNOWLEDGE A DIFFICULT TRUTH AND THEN STATE WHY CUSTOMERS NEED NOT WORRY ABOUT IT

- The fact is, all technology requires downtime. That's why our technology services have triple backup.
- Just because you aren't our largest client doesn't mean you aren't important.
- Our hourly consulting rate is 200% more. But we do 300% more.
- If you're not absolutely satisfied, we'll give you a full refund—no questions asked.

- Chances are, you will catch at least one cold this winter. We can help you beat those odds.
- Are you used to surly service people? We only hire people we'd want our kids to work for.

11. SUMMARIZE YOUR MAIN PERSUASIVE ARGUMENTS

- There are three reasons to choose us as your painters: we only work on one job at a time, we have great references, and we clean up after ourselves.
- In a nutshell, our software is so intuitive that your newest employee can be using it within two hours.
- We started our first hospice over 40 years ago in our own house. Today, there are over 200 hospices worldwide.
- We are the area's most popular news channel. That's what the ratings say.

Four Creative Approaches to Writing Body Copy for Brochures

1. LIST MULTIPLE FEATURES, SERVICES, AND/OR BENEFITS

- Our maintenance services include: interior and exterior painting, minor construction and remodeling, floor waxing, basic cleaning, kitchen cleaning, bathroom cleaning, tree trimming, mowing, equipment purchasing and maintenance, electrical repair, and plumbing repair.

- We have over 150 local agents in over 70 countries. And they are backed by our 24/7 toll-free emergency service hotline. Our hotline operators speak over 50 languages.

- There are multiple advantages to using a single integrated marketing firm to design all your communications: 1) we are not hammers who see every problem as a nail, so you can trust our recommendations; 2) all your communications will work together to build brand equity; 3) we can avoid costly duplication and overlap of media; and 4) you can simplify your life.

2. PROVIDE REASONS TO BELIEVE YOUR MAIN CLAIM

- Our client list includes five of the ten most profitable and fastest-growing companies within their respective categories.

- Over 80% of all transactions in the banking industry use our open-source formats. This ensures compatibility and ease of transaction.

- Of the last 2,000 employees who left our company to work for our competitors, 1,835 asked for their old jobs back—and 1,524 were willing to come back at reduced pay.

3. GIVE AN EXAMPLE

The best examples are mini-stories involving people in problem situations who were helped by your product or service. The more vivid, detailed, and dramatic, the better.

- The client's data showed that 15% of the products shipped to customers were being returned for various problems. Our analysis traced 80% of these problems to errors made in manufacturing on Mondays and Fridays. We recommended increasing work hours on Tuesday through Thursday and offering employees bonus pay for Mondays and Fridays. The result was a 73% decline in returned products.

- Susan's mother had passed away years before. Susan's father didn't understand much about how to put together a good wedding, especially details like dresses and flowers and food. So we assigned an in-house expert to guide him through all the choices and the costs. The result was a wedding that, as Susan said, "My mother would have been proud of."

- Our chocolates are all handmade under the supervision of the owner. She travels the world to select the cacao beans that have the right taste, based on the soil in which they are grown. This is similar to how winemakers select grapes.

4. USE PHOTOS/ILLUSTRATIONS AND CAPTIONS

- (beautiful color photo of artistic print) Caption: All our prints are limited-edition signed originals.

- (photo of president receiving industry award) Caption: President Christopher Woods receives the Lifetime Achievement Award from the International Association of Plumbing Contractors.

- (two diagrams of a manufacturing process: a complex "before" diagram and a simplified "after" diagram) Caption: Before and after our design process review. We were able to reduce the number of steps in product manufacturing from 112 to 52, improving quality and lowering costs.

Posters and Flyers

Most posters and flyers consist of eight parts. Except for the main visual and the logo, all the parts are words and phrases.

1. Main visual
2. Headline
3. Subhead
4. Basic details: date, time, location, price
5. Highlighted details
6. Call to action
7. Logo or name
8. Slogan

Don't expect people to read all of your poster or flyer. People scan, then decide whether or not to read. As a result, some parts of your poster/flyer are more important than others: people first look at the main visual, the headline, and the logo or name. They then decide, within a half second, whether to invest any time and energy in the rest of the ad.

So pay extra attention to making these elements dominant, relevant, and unexpected. If people decide to read your poster or flyer, they will next look at the basic details line and then the call to action. Only then will they actually read the remaining words.

Above all, keep your poster or flyer as brief as possible. Avoid writing full sentences.

Time-Saving Tip: You can use almost the same visuals, headline, and other information for your posters and flyers as for your print ads and your brochures. It's more efficient and it's more effective for building "brand equity."

Dos and Don'ts

- Do use graphic design to create a hierarchy of dominance to guide the readers' eyes from the most important thing, to the second-most, to the third-most, and so forth.

- Don't make the readers work hard or think too much to find what is important on the page.

- Do use powerful selling words, like *free*, *new*, *now*, *introducing*, and *save*.

- Do avoid general and abstract words like *quality*, *convenience*, *advanced*, *partnership*, and *solutions*.

- Don't reverse out the type at all (white letters on a black background). It can reduce readability as much as 60% and make it tough on people who may want to take your flyer and write on it.

- Do make one main point per flyer. Lead with your strongest reason to care.

- Make sure it is easy to spot the basic details—date, time, location, and price.

- If you can afford it, take advantage of color to attract attention.

- List highlights in bullet form for easy reading. Don't write paragraphs of words.

- Do make sure you include a call to action. It can increase results as much as 20%.

- Don't imitate what your competitors are doing. Do stand out.

Nine Steps to Creating a Poster or a Flyer

To create your poster or flyer, create the eight pieces and then put them all together.

Step 1. Select a photo or illustration.

Here are some classic subjects for your flyer/poster photo or illustration:

- A special event
- Symbols of enjoyment: balloons, music, entertainment, games
- Your product or service
- A person using your product or service
- The benefit of your product or service
- The problem your product or service solves
- A satisfied customer
- A map showing your location
- A picture of your store or facility
- A dramatic demonstration of your product or service
- A cutaway view of the inside of your product

Step 2. Create a headline.

The headline should state your single most important point. Consider including your name or the name of your event in your headline. Strongly consider using a promotional offer or news approach in your poster or flyer. (Use the creative approaches presented in Chapter 2, pages 21–27.)

Step 3. Create a subhead.

The subhead should state your second-most important point. Make sure the headline and subhead don't duplicate each other. Use type size and placement to make sure the headline is read first and the subhead is read second. Your subhead can also be your company name, listed as an event sponsor. (Use the creative approaches presented in Chapter 2, page 28.)

Step 4. Create a summary of the basic facts: date, time, location, and price.

Try to be as brief as possible, so that the information can be large enough to read easily from a distance.

- New summer hours: 9 AM–9 PM Mon–Sun
  1234 Main Street (across from Meadowview Mall)
  50% off all of last year's paint colors (good until Aug. 1)
  Call: XXX-XXX-XXXX
- Grand Opening Celebration
  Saturday and Sunday, April 23–24
  10:30 AM to 5:00 PM.
  Downtown near Main Ave. and State St.
  Free parking
- Free Insurance Seminar
  Westin Hotel Grand Ballroom
  Sugarland, Texas (I-10, Exit 43 South)
  Admission: $50 per person
  Group Discounts Available
  Call: 1-800-FREEINSURE
  Visit: www.freeinsure.com
  Seating is limited

Step 5. Highlight details.

Choose one to three details that make your offer particularly compelling or enjoyable. Write them as individual bullets, as briefly as possible.

- Speaker: Barry Callen, author of the best-selling *Perfect Phrases for Sales and Marketing Copy*
- Free toys, games, clowns, balloons, music, and prizes
- Free discounts to seniors
- Thousands of shoes. Hundreds of famous brands. All 50% off.
- Live broadcast with WFGM Radio D.J. Killerdog!
- Enter to Win our Raffle: Prizes include one year of free DVD rentals.

Step 6. Create a call to action.

Often this can be added to your date, time, place, and location. If tickets or RSVP are required, make sure to indicate that. (Use the creative approaches in Chapter 2, pages 30–31 to create a better call to action.)

Step 7. Place your name or logo.

In general, you should place your logo in the lower right of your poster or flyer or in the bottom at the center. (For a better name, use the creative tips in Chapter 2, pages 7–11.)

Step 8. Add your slogan.

Your slogan should generally run either just below your logo or at the bottom of your poster or flyer. (For a better slogan, use the creative tips in Chapter 2, pages 13–19.)

Step 9. Assemble all the pieces.

Use type size, boldness, and placement to make sure there is a clear hierarchy of dominance: a most important thing, a second-most important thing, and so on. This will help guide the readers' eyes to the most important things in your poster or flyer. Be sure to leave a lot of white space. Break up large blocks of words into smaller blocks.

Billboards

There are four components of a billboard:

1. Main visual
2. Headline
3. Logo or name
4. Slogan … or … Call to action … or neither

Drivers rarely spend more than seven seconds reading a billboard. There are two secrets to an effective billboard. One is to have an unexpected or compelling visual to grab attention. The other is to have a message so simple that it requires only a headline to communicate. The total number of words on your billboard, including your name and tagline, should never exceed 12.

Time-Saving Tip: You can use essentially the exact same visuals and headline on your billboard as in your print materials. Again, that repetition helps build "brand equity."

The core message may be the same in both media, but you must ruthlessly edit your billboard to be as brief as possible. Sometimes it's enough just to get your name out there.

Dos and Don'ts

■ Do choose a compelling visual. It should be a quick clear read that requires no guessing. It should be relevant and unexpected.

■ Don't exceed 12 words total on your billboard, including your name and slogan. Drivers simply don't have time to read more than that.

■ Do use graphic design to create a strong hierarchy of dominance to guide the readers' eyes from the most important thing, to the second-most, to the third-most, and so forth.

Tactics for Print and Display Media

- Don't make the readers work hard or think too much to translate what you are trying to say. Be clear.
- Do use powerful selling words, like *free*, *new*, *now*, *introducing*, and *save*.
- Do avoid general and abstract words like *quality*, *convenience*, *advanced*, *partnership*, and *solutions*.
- Don't reverse out the type in your body copy (white letters on a black background). It can reduce readability as much as 60%.
- Do make one main point per billboard—and no more.
- Don't slap sponsor logos on your billboard.

Five Steps to Creating a Billboard

To create your billboard, create the four pieces and then put them all together.

Step 1. Select a photo or illustration.

If your words are the most important part of your billboard, you can go without a visual. Otherwise, you are better off having a compelling visual. Here are some classic subjects for your photo or illustration:

- Your product or service
- A person using your product or service
- The benefit of your product or service
- The problem your product or service solves
- A satisfied customer
- A map showing your location
- A picture of your store or facility
- A dramatic demonstration of your product or service
- A cutaway view of the inside of your product
- Animals
- Children
- Beautiful women and handsome men
- Tasty-looking food
- Refreshing drink
- Celebrities (get legal approval)

Step 2. Create a headline.

The headline should state your single most important point. Keep it short and sweet. (Use the creative approaches presented in Chapter 2, pages 21–27.)

Step 3. Place your name or logo.

If you use a headline, you should place your logo in the lower right of your billboard or in the bottom at the center. (For a better name, use the creative approaches in Chapter 2, pages 7–11.)

- If your logo is your headline or your visual, place it directly in the center of the billboard, as large as you can make it.
- If your logo is complex, consider using your name spelled in type instead.
- This is no place to be formal. If you can abbreviate your name in any way, do it. For example, "Holy Cross Health Services and Hospital" can be abridged on a billboard as "Holy Cross Health" or "Holy Cross Hospital."

Step 4: Add your slogan or ... a call to action ... or neither.

If using a slogan would push the number of words on your billboard over 12, then leave it off. If your slogan is so good you don't want to leave it off, make your slogan the headline. (For a better slogan, use the creative approaches in Chapter 2, pages 13–19.) If you have room for both a headline and a slogan, the slogan should generally run either just below your logo or at the bottom of your ad.

In general, it's too wordy to use both a slogan and a call to action. If you use a call to action, keep it very, very brief and don't use a slogan. If you use a slogan, forgo a call to action.

The fewer words the better. If you can communicate your message with just a visual, a headline, and your name, do it. To get ideas for additional calls to action, see the creative approaches presented in Chapter 2, pages 30–31.

Step 5. Assemble all the pieces.

Use type size, boldness, and placement to make sure there is a clear hierarchy of dominance: a most important thing, a second-most important thing, and so on. This will help guide the readers' eyes to the most important things in your ad. Be sure to leave a lot of white space. Again, no more than 12 words on your billboard.

Yellow Pages Ads

The most effective Yellow Pages ads consist of seven parts. Except for the main visual and the logo (and possibly a map), all the parts are words and phrases.

1. Main visual
2. Headline
3. Subhead
4. Useful information and/or points of difference
5. Stimulus for immediate action (call)
6. Logo or name
7. Slogan

Most people reading the Yellow Pages have already decided to make a purchase. So the primary purpose of a Yellow Pages ad is to get them to pay attention to your ad instead of those of your competitors and then get them to choose your business over your competitors.

Unlike most advertising, and particularly unlike billboards, there is very little value to having lots of empty space in your ad. In fact you should cram your ad with as much useful and differentiating information as possible. Be sure however, that you prioritize the information using visuals, type sizes, and placement.

Because people reading your ad are ready to buy, advertising your name for them to recall later is less important than promising you can solve their problem right now. Don't be afraid to communicate your information in a way that invokes emotion.

Dos and Don'ts

- Do use a visual to dominate their attention on the page. Make sure the visual is not just decoration or an icon. Make sure it gets the reader to feel something.

- After the visual, make your headline the dominant element in the ad. The headline should either promise the immediate solution to a problem or prove how you differ from competitors.
- After the headline, make sure your phone number is the dominant element. It is even more important than your name and logo. Give them an incentive to call right away.
- Do use powerful selling words, like *free, new, now, introducing*, and *save*.
- Do avoid general and abstract words like *quality, convenience, advanced, partnership*, and *solutions*.
- Don't reverse out the type in your body copy (white letters on a black background). It can reduce readability as much as 60%.
- Do cram your ad with services and features, with reasons to believe your main promise, with reasons to call now, and with ways that you are different from competitors.
- Don't imitate what your competitors are doing. Do stand out.
- Don't use visuals for decoration only, such as borders, frames, or icons. Instead, use visuals that communicate information, differentiate your ad from the competition, or engage the reader emotionally.
- Don't make any claims you can't back up. Negative word of mouth travels fast.

Eight Steps to Creating a Yellow Pages Ad

To create your Yellow Pages ad, create the seven pieces of your ad and then put them all together.

Step 1. Select a photo or illustration.

Here are some classic subjects for your photo or illustration:

- You, the owner
- Your product or service
- The tools you use to fix things
- A person using your product or service
- The benefit or results of your product or service
- The problem your product or service solves
- A satisfied customer
- A map showing your location
- A picture of your store or facility
- A dramatic demonstration of your product or service
- A cutaway view of the inside of your product
- Animals
- Children
- Beautiful women and handsome men
- Tasty-looking food
- Refreshing drink
- Celebrities (get legal approval)
- People having fun

Step 2. Create a headline.

Yellow Pages customers are ready to buy, so you don't need to make them aware of your name for later. Your headline should either promise an immediate solution to a customer problem or clearly state how you are different from your competitors. Yellow

Pages headlines should be as brief and as emotionally engaging as possible. See pages 77–82 for phrases for headlines.

Step 3. Create a subhead.

The subhead should state your second-most important point. Make sure the headline and subhead don't duplicate each other. Use type size and placement to make sure the headline is read first and the subhead is read second. Use the headline creative approaches listed on pages 77–82 to generate your subhead. Try to use one kind of approach for the headline and a different approach for the subhead. Here are three examples:

■ **Headline:** State a tangible benefit involving time, money, safety, or ease:
Reduce your chances of environmental fines.

■ **Subhead:** Summarize your main persuasive arguments:
We sell the world's cleanest fuel.

■ **Headline:** State whom your company serves, what you do, and how you are different:
Our insurance inspectors would rather prevent accidents than cover them.

■ **Subhead:** State an emotional benefit that fulfills a desire or alleviates a fear:
We worry so you don't have to.

■ **Headline:** Use humor:
If you don't have a good accountant, may we suggest a good lawyer?
Subhead: Use a customer testimonial:
"I trust their accuracy." Dr. Mark Marx, Professor of Accounting, University of Business

Step 4. List useful information, points of difference, or reasons to believe.

Use an extremely abbreviated form of writing. Use bullets or lists or phrases.

- Over 50 Fortune 500 clients.
- Used by 40% of all insurance customers.
- Less than a .00001% error rate.
- Recommended by nine out of ten brides.
- Services include marketing strategy, media strategy and buying, new media, graphic design, advertising, public relations, and broadcast and print production.
- Over 30 service locations worldwide.
- Make instant changes. Integrate care among departments. Prevent drug reactions. Improve cash flow.
- Authorized dealer of 20 top brands.
- Area's oldest and largest car dealership.

Step 5. Get potential customers to call immediately.

- Call toll-free 1-800-XXX-XXXX.
- Call 24/7 for instant service.
- Call anytime M–F, 9 AM–5 PM.
- Call on Tuesdays and save 10%.
- Reserve space now. Hurry—seating is limited.
- First come, first serve. Call now.
- Call 1-800-ACT-NOWW.
- First-time customers save up to 50% with this coupon.
- Get a free safety inspection with every oil change.
- Buy one, get the second half-price, if you order by phone.
- The first 50 callers also get a free T-shirt.
- Two free lottery tickets with every purchase over $50.

- Sign up today for our rewards program and get preferred customer benefits.
- Call the only area certified and bonded roofers.

Step 6. Place your name or logo.

In general, you should place your logo in the lower right of your ad or in the bottom at the center. Your name is least important in a Yellow Pages ad, because your customers are more interested in solving their problem now than in remembering your name later. Therefore, you don't need to put your name in large print or in a prominent place.

By the way, it is not a bad idea to choose a name that alphabetically causes you to be listed first, such as AAAAA-Auto Repair or Aardvark Painting. (For a better name, use the creative tips in Chapter 2, pages 7–11.)

Step 7. Add your slogan.

Your slogan should generally run either just below your logo or at the bottom of your ad. (For a better slogan, use the creative approaches in Chapter 2, pages 13–19.)

Step 8. Assemble all the pieces.

Use type size, boldness, and placement to make sure there is a clear hierarchy of dominance: a most important thing, a second-most important thing, and so on. This will help guide the readers' eyes to the most important things in your ad. Feel free to fill your entire ad wall to wall with information, as long as it is easy to read and useful.

17 Creative Approaches to Writing a Yellow Pages Headline

1. STATE A TANGIBLE BENEFIT INVOLVING TIME, MONEY, SAFETY, OR EASE

- Our cosmetology graduates earn 20% more.
- Reduce your chances of environmental fines.
- Let our tools do more of the work.
- Become headache-free in five treatments.
- Decrease employee turnover 15%.

2. STATE AN EMOTIONAL BENEFIT THAT FULFILLS A DESIRE OR ALLEVIATES A FEAR

- Your face can look ten years younger.
- Never worry about a broken garage door again.
- Give your family a vacation that makes the world a better place.
- Put your home equity to work so you don't have to.
- We can help you get into your dream college.
- We worry so you don't have to.

3. STATE A PROBLEM AND PROVIDE A SOLUTION

- Put an end to home allergens with one phone call.
- Too many home repairs? Consider condo living.
- Need a ride fast? Our taxi can be there in minutes.
- If you are losing market share, our research can help.
- Old paint and chemicals recycled cheap.

4. PROVIDE A DEMONSTRATION

- Even under four feet of snow, our snow blower clears the way.

- She lost 100 pounds in 40 days!
- If you can read this ad, you can learn to fly an airplane.
- This man built this entire house with our rental equipment.

5. FLAG THE PROSPECT

- Thinking about adoption? We have international connections.
- A health clinic for gays, lesbians, and bisexuals.
- If you appreciate fine wine, you'll love our weekly tasting parties.
- Does your child suffer from ADD?
- We specialize in Medicare services for seniors.
- Serving the men and women in our armed forces since 1942.
- ¡El dinero no compra el amor! (foreign language)

6. ASK A QUESTION

Use the five W's—who, what, when, where, and why—to provoke your reader.

- Guess who does the most home loans in our city?
- When can you call us? 24/7!
- Why do we triple-wrap and air-cool our meat deliveries?
- How can we offer you twice as much for half the usual price?

7. OFFER SAVINGS

- Why hunt for sales? Our prices are always the lowest.
- The lowest price—or we'll refund the difference.

8. STATE HOW YOU ARE DIFFERENT FROM THE COMPETITION

- The area's oldest continuous water heating supplier.

- The area's only certified Maytag Repair Center.
- Exclusive purveyor of Up-Zero Freezers.
- No one else can match our prices.
- We can be there while you're still on hold with the other guys.
- The largest selection of merchandise in the greater metro area.
- Not every mechanic is ASE-certified. But all ours are.

9. USE HUMOR

- If you don't have a good accountant, may we suggest a good lawyer?
- Our printing quality is a lot better than this ad.
- You didn't start your business to change the copier paper. But we did.
- Is your carpenter's idea of a cost estimate to add a zero and multiply by two?
- Ophthalmologists with vision.

10. USE AN EXPERT ENDORSEMENT

Make sure you get a signed legal release with permission to use the individual or organization's name.

- All our plumbers are nationally certified Master Plumbers.
- "I bought my fly shoes at the Shoe Fly." Tommy 'Too-Big' Balanka, Leopards forward
- As seen on TV.
- Named the city's number-one burger joint by Eatery Magazine.
- Rated among America's ten best archery ranges by the National Archery Association.

11. USE A CUSTOMER TESTIMONIAL

Look for extreme customer behavior or for individuals with great credibility. Make sure you get a signed legal release with permission to use the individual's name.

- "We drive over 50 miles just to get our car fixed there." Wanda and Faber Lewis
- "I don't trust my pets to just any groomer." Heidi Fillena, dog and cat owner
- Cal O'Riley has been eating our salmon every Friday night for 23 years.
- "I trust their motives." Dr. Maria Verdadera, Professor of Ethical Studies, University of Granger

12. WORK WITH AN OBJECTION

Acknowledge a typical bias or opinion or problem in the headline and then refute it in the body copy.

- Not all mechanics are out to rip you off.
- The problem with used car salesmen is that they are all liars. Right?
- Most meditation is New Age wishful thinking. But we can prove it heals.
- 50% of all doctors are below average. By any measure our doctors are in the top 10%.
- Computers can be really stupid. So we include a free human expert with each one.

13. STATE WHY POTENTIAL CUSTOMERS SHOULD CARE ABOUT YOUR BUSINESS

- If you like on-time delivery, you'll love our courier service.
- Can't afford to lose one minute of factory downtime?

- Is your business failing? Don't fail to call the turnaround experts.
- Nothing is more important than knowing your loved ones will be taken care of.
- Identify and address the system errors that give you the biggest headaches.

14. STATE WHOM YOUR COMPANY SERVES, WHAT YOU DO, AND HOW YOU ARE DIFFERENT

- Our insurance inspectors would rather prevent accidents than cover them.
- We only auction items that appeal to individuals with taste and resources.
- Can't get a loan? We can turn your car into your bank.
- We stand for one thing: accuracy. All your payroll and vendors checks are 99.9% accurate.
- We're not like most corporate law firms. If we can keep you out of court, we will.
- We understand the needs of military personnel, because we employ only former military personnel.
- We live to find ways for you to pay less income tax.

15. SHOW YOU UNDERSTAND THE CUSTOMERS' POINT OF VIEW BY DESCRIBING IT

- You hate waiting for delivery confirmation. So do we. We track online real time.
- If you think most gift stores are the same, you're right. But we're different.
- We understand that one wrong purchase can ruin a whole career.
- You don't have to be rich to get our best service.

16. ACKNOWLEDGE A DIFFICULT TRUTH AND THEN STATE WHY CUSTOMERS NEED NOT WORRY ABOUT IT

- You can't trust most body shop estimates. So ours are done independently.
- Our hydraulic systems cost up to 10% more—but they last 230% longer.
- If you're not absolutely satisfied, we'll give you a full refund, no questions asked.
- Are you used to less than perfect installation? We double-check our work.

17. SUMMARIZE YOUR MAIN PERSUASIVE ARGUMENTS

- Why choose us? Only 1% administrative costs, global reach, and real-time status reporting.
- In a nutshell, our people care more.
- We've been designing retail outlets for over 20 years.
- Over 300 locations citywide.
- We sell the world's cleanest fuel.

Classified Ads

Classified newspaper ad readers are already interested in considering what you have to sell, so you don't have to convince them, for example, to buy a house or hire a builder or get a job. Instead, you have to get them to pay attention to *your* ad and decide that *your* offer is worth checking out: you want them to buy *your* house, hire *you* as a builder, and apply for a job at *your* company.

Here are the five components of a classified ad:

1. Main visual
2. Headline
3. Useful details, accurate descriptions, unique differences
4. Price
5. Phone number

Some buyers shop visually, some read only the headlines, some look only at the prices, and some are searching for that something different or special or unique. Your best bet is to appeal to all four types of readers with a useful visual that draws attention, a headline that gets right to the point, an appealing price, and an offer that is unique. Always put your phone number at the bottom so they can call right away. Your goal is to generate the call so that they will find out more.

Dos and Don'ts

- Do use a visual that shows what you are selling and how it is different or better.
- Do use your headline to highlight what you are selling and to highlight its single most desirable and unique feature.
- Do look at other ads to decide what minimum information must be included. For example, when advertising a house, you should include the number of bedrooms and bathrooms.

- Do use descriptive details to briefly highlight key features, benefits, differences, and surprises.
- Do sprinkle in a few emotional or sensory adjectives like "charming bungalow" or "fun workplace" or "clean and neat" and let the reader imagine the rest.
- Do use large or bold type to capture attention.
- Do put your phone number at the bottom of the ad.
- Do highlight the price.
- Do give people a reason to call right away, such as "First offer accepted" or "Free estimate."
- Don't highlight your name. You want people to call right away to buy your product or service, not remember your company name for later.
- Don't use abbreviations the average reader won't understand.
- Do change your ad if it's not working. Try different approaches. In some categories, such as employment or houses for sale, running the same ad for a while is a sign that something's wrong.
- Do continue to run your ad if it's working. Some classified ads have run effectively for decades.
- Do test your results. Most newspapers can help you do what is called split-run copy testing. This is the simplest way of developing the most successful ad. You experiment by running two ads, the control and a version with one difference, with different phone numbers. Determine whether any difference between the two response rates is statistically significant. First test where you place the ad. Then test the offer (price, product, benefit, promotion). Then test the words. Then test the layout.

Tactics for Print and Display Media

■ Do ask your local newspaper for help in crafting your ad. But make sure your ad stands out or is different in some way from the vast majority of ads.

Classified Ad Examples

1. SERVICES

(VISUAL: *COMPLEX CURVING GOTHIC MANSION ROOF*)

Historically Accurate Custom Roofing

Historical Society references. We focus on one job at a time.
First-come first-serve scheduling. Now reserving for August.

608-XXX-XXXX

(VISUAL: *DOGHOUSE WITH ROOF AND HAPPY DOG*)

NO ROOFING JOB TOO SMALL.

Over 20 years' experience. All jobs guaranteed.
All roofers bonded & friendly.

919-XXX-XXXX

EMERGENCY Roof Repair

Same-day temporary weather protection.
Available evenings/weekends.
Free estimates. 24/7 hotline. Call now to prevent
serious water damage.

515-XXX-XXXX

2. EMPLOYMENT

Need an extra $10,000?

Try Food Service Sales
Set your own hours. Part-time/full-time. No previous
experience necessary.

768-XXX-XXXX

LIFETIME CAREER OPPTY in Food Service Sales

Join the nation's largest most successful food purveyor.
Sales are up 50% this year. Promotions. Benefits. Insurance.
Bonuses. 768-XXX-XXXX

Experienced Food Service Sales Wanted
Call on our largest accounts. Exclusive new territory.
Salary based on experience. Straight commission.
212-XXX-XXXX

3. REAL ESTATE

(VISUAL: *SKYLIGHT WITH SKY*)
Spacious LOFT Near Arts District $450,000
Historic brick-lined Otterbach Brewery. High ceilings.
Natural oak floors.
Modern heat, elect., appliances. Recently renovated.
5 bdrm/2 bath. Heated underground parking.
Call Melissa Baxter at Arthouse Realty.
707-XXX-XXXX

(VISUAL: *FIREPLACE WITH FIRE*)
Cozy bungalow perfect for couple
20,000 sq. ft. 3 bdrm/1.5 bath. Basement storage.
Wraparound porch. 2-car garage. $160,000.
SHOWING SUN. Noon–5 PM
FSBO 402-XXX-XXXX

(VISUAL: *FOREST LAKE WITH DOCK AND ROWBOAT*)
NEW LISTING! 40,000 sq. ft. LOG CABIN w/private lake
Privacy ensured with 10-acre forest, winding driveway. Apple
grove. River access. Good fishing/hunting. Fireplace. 6
bdrm/5 bath. $860,000 minimum or first offer.
Represented by North Woods Realty
Serious inquiries only. 1-800-XXX-XXXX

Chapter 4
Tactics for Radio and Television Sales and Marketing Copy

Live-Read Announcer Radio Ad

A live-read radio commercial is a set of words read by radio station announcers from a radio script you provide. This type of radio commercial is the least expensive to produce, requires no expensive music or sound effects, and does not require a professional level of creative writing ability. Best of all, you can change your radio commercial to take advantage of current news, weather, and local references, just by writing a new script.

Most radio commercials are either 30 or 60 seconds long. Be sure you put a stopwatch to your finished script and read it out loud. Most live-read radio commercials are actually prerecorded and radio stations won't run a commercial that goes over time by even a quarter second. To play it safe, plan for your script to take about 26 seconds to read for a 30-second commercial or 54 seconds for a 60-second commercial. This will give the announcer time to provide dramatic pauses and changes of pace for emphasis, and time to use a friendly relaxing conversational style instead of an irritating racing shout. In general, you are better off buying a 60-second radio commercial.

Use words that are short and easy to say. Avoid lots of "S" words in a row. ("She sells seashells by the seashore" would be hard to read out loud.) The letter "S" also causes lisping and is hard to say. Try to avoid a lot of words with the letter "P" also. They tend to produce an irritating "pop" into the microphone. "Peter Piper picked a peck of pickled peppers" would not be a good radio sentence to write.

Radio listeners are usually not in a position to act on your offer right away. So it is important that they remember your name. It is generally a good idea to mention your product or company name at the very beginning, in the middle, and at the very end. A general guideline is to use the name three times in a 30-second ad and at least five times in a 60-second ad. Don't be afraid to repeat your name twice at the end.

Radio listeners tune in for news and entertainment, not commercials. Make sure your commercial is either useful or enjoyable, and try to make it as unexpected as possible in order to get their attention. Radio listeners are often doing other things while they are listening, like driving or working, so make sure your message is extremely clear and simple. Some repetition of main points helps.

Six Steps to Creating a Live-Read Radio Announcer Ad

Step 1. Get attention. Create a provocative opening to capture attention.

Step 2. Increase involvement. Paint a sensory picture or tell a story to emotionally hook the listeners.

Step 3. Prove belief. Prove that the listeners can believe what you are saying.

Step 4. Call to action. Ask the listeners to do something.

Step 5. Remember the name. Make sure the listeners remember your name.

Step 6. Write the script. Assemble the parts into a whole.

Time-Saving Tip: You can use almost the exact same information for both your live-read radio script and your locally produced TV script: same opening, interest, proof, call to action, and name. Doing so saves time and helps reinforce your message and make it more memorable. This is "integrated marketing communications" and it helps build "brand equity" for a higher long-term return on your communications investment.

While you communicate the same core message in both media, in radio you have only audio, so you may want to provide more verbal explanation and details in your radio commercial.

Dos and Don'ts

- Do type your script and double-check it for factual errors. Triple-check all contact information.
- Don't exaggerate or make false claims of superiority or you will open yourself up to potential lawsuits and generate negative word of mouth among customers.
- Don't make superlative claims like *always, never, guaranteed, promise, forever, permanently, unquestionably, absolutely, the best, better than, superior to, the only, exclusively,* etc. unless you can prove them.
- Do make sure your script takes less than 30 seconds or less

than 60 seconds to read at a normal pace. Aim for 26 seconds or 54 seconds. Use a stopwatch.

- Do favor using a 60-second ad. It enables you to communicate more information and it is generally a better media value.

- Do make your opening *surprising, unexpected, newsworthy, entertaining,* or *useful.*

- Don't use circus promotion language like *amazing, greatest,* and *unbelievable* or general or abstract words like *quality, convenience, advanced, partnership,* and *solutions.*

- Do mention your company name two to three times. The best times are at the beginning, in the middle, and at the end.

- Do repeat your phone number at least twice. This will give listeners time to write it down.

- Do make one main point per commercial—and then prove it.

- Don't make your commercial a long list of claims. People won't remember them.

- Do make sure you include one simple call to action.

- Don't imitate what your competitors are doing, especially your largest competitors, or people will confuse your commercials for theirs. Then you've wasted your money.

- Don't write tongue-twisters or use lots of "S" words in a row. They are hard to say.

- Don't use lots of words that begin with "P." They tend to make a popping sound.

- Do spell out numbers for easy reading. For example, write, "Call one-two-three, four-five-six-seven" instead of "Call 123-4567."

- Don't break words at the end of a typed line. The break makes them harder to read without pausing in the wrong place.

- Do provide phonetic descriptions of names that are not intuitive to pronounce. For example, write, "Call Bob Schmermerhorn (Schmur Mer Horn)."
- Do write to be clear, rather than to be clever. Say something worth hearing.
- Do make sure you are prepared to handle a sudden increase in store visits or call volume.

Creative Tip: Choose a single perspective—"you" or "we" or "they"—and stick with your choice.

You can write your phrases from three perspectives. You can use the first person (we), the second person (you), or the third person (they). Whichever perspective you choose, be consistent throughout your commercial or you will confuse the listeners.

Here are examples of the three perspectives.

- *first person:*
  At House Healers, *we* guarantee every repair.
- *second person:*
  You will love the fact that every repair is guaranteed.
- *third person:*
  He likes the fact that all our repairs are guaranteed.
  Everyone likes the fact that all our repairs are guaranteed.
  Homeowners like the fact that all our repairs are guaranteed.
  They like the fact that all our repairs are guaranteed.
  All repairs are guaranteed.

Choose the perspective that seems the most natural to you and be consistent throughout your script. Remember that someone else will be reading your script.

To create your live-read radio commercial, create the five pieces of your ad and then put them all together into a script.

Step One. Get Attention: 16 Ways to Create a Provocative Live-Read Opening

1. ANNOUNCE NEWS

- Don't miss our once-a-year half-price sale!
- We're open 24 hours all Labor Day Weekend.
- Introducing a brand-new way to replace thinning hair.

2. REFER TO A CURRENT EVENT

- Buy two pairs of pants, get the third free during our back-to-school sale.
- This Juneteenth, get your barbeque sauce from a national award-winning chef.
- A portion of all our September sales will go to support the widows and orphans of the brave 911 firefighters.

3. REFER TO THE LOCAL AREA

- The maple trees are almost ready to tap, and we've got the buckets you need.
- If you live in the greater Biggtown area, here's important news.
- Madison is Badger country, and we've got the T-shirts and hats to prove it.

4. REFER TO THE WEATHER

- Cascade Mountain just got ten inches of fresh powder.
- It's almost time to get your car winterized.
- The wind is a comfortable five miles an hour, and the lake is smooth as glass.

5. CREATE URGENCY

- Before you take your family on summer vacation, better get your brakes checked.

- Hurry! The sale ends at midnight tonight, and it won't be back for another year.
- Hurricane season is almost upon us. Time to stock up on emergency supplies.

6. USE A SURPRISING FACT

- Your family may be catching colds from the germs on your kitchen counter.
- The dust in your home is … yuck … mostly skin cells that have been shed by you.
- Most vacuum cleaners simply move the dirt around. They don't get rid of it.

7. OFFER A PROMOTION

- Get a free tire inspection with every alignment.
- The first fifty callers to order fruitcake will get a three-piece box of chocolates, absolutely free.
- Announcing our Couldn't Think of a Catchy Name Sale.

8. FLAG YOUR CUSTOMER

- If you're thinking about a backyard pool, now is the time to visit our showroom.
- Have you been in a motorcycle accident recently?
- If you like original artwork, you'll love our Starving Artist Exhibition.

9. CONTRADICT A BELIEF

- Our lawyers are no joke.
- Introducing a health care system with absolutely no paper-work—guaranteed.
- Forget everything you know about car mechanics.

10. STATE A BENEFIT

- Motivate your employees to go the extra mile.
- Getting away from it all is just a two-hour drive away.
- Turn your trash into treasure from home … online!

11. TELL HOW YOU ARE UNIQUE

Make sure you can prove your unique claim.

- The founder of Honey Dew Farms was born in Bavaria and raised by beekeepers.
- We are the only area dealer certified to repair Superva Computers.
- Clintonville's oldest and largest farm equipment dealership is having a 50th anniversary sale.

12. STATE A PROBLEM TO SOLVE

- Free yourself from credit card debt.
- Get rid of aging spots without surgery.
- Let us sort out all the college scholarship red tape for you.

13. ASK A QUESTION

- When was the last time you were treated like a queen?
- Got mice? Get rid of them humanely, once and for all.
- What would you do to improve your home, if you knew you had the money?
- How much do you think it would cost to fly to Europe this summer?

14. USE AN UNUSUAL WORD

- Yikes! Did you forget to pay your taxes?
- Yippee! That's what folks say when they ride our motor scooters.

- There's a word for ice cream this fresh. And that word is "Mmmmmm."

15. USE YOUR CATEGORY DESCRIPTOR

This helps integrate your communications for a higher return on investment. To create a better business category descriptor, see the "Slogans, Theme Lines, and Taglines" section of Chapter 2, pages 13–19.

- When you need emergency furnace and air-conditioning repair, call A-1 A.C.
- We specialize in custom-building private homes, including summer cottages.
- Homemade pies served fresh daily. That's all we do.

16. USE YOUR PRINT AD HEADLINE

This helps integrate your communications for a higher return on investment. To create a better headline, see the "Headlines" section of Chapter 2, pages 21–27.

Step Two. Increase Involvement: Eight Ways to Emotionally Hook Listeners

Now that you've gotten the attention of listeners, you want to interest them in finding out more about your story. You want to get them emotionally engaged. The best way to do this is by using your words to trigger their imagination. Help them see what you are saying in their mind's eye. This is the place for drama, entertainment, sensory detail, experiences, and stories.

1. TELL A STORY

- Bob and Carol Owens arrived back home from their annual family reunion to find that their home wasn't there. The night before, a tornado completely swept everything away. They immediately called their insurance agent, Mary Quintanos. Within one hour, they had a free hotel room for the week, a thermos of hot coffee, and a check for $200,000.

- When Jamar Washington was seven, he liked to take apart lawn mower engines. By the time he was 12, he could also put them back together. When he was 18, he repaired his first sports car—a 1965 green Mustang convertible. After that he was hooked. Ten years later, he opened the area's first sports car repair service, Jamar's SportCar Shop, and he's probably fixed over 2,000 sports cars since then.

- As a young woman, Henrietta had three strikes against her. She hadn't completed high school, she had only worked in a variety of menial low-skill low-pay jobs, and she was in a wheelchair. She found the courage to attend her first class at University Community College, and we helped her find the scholarships and work-study programs to pay for it. Today, she is earning a six-figure income in a state government job and just got promoted to supervisor.

2. QUOTE A PERSON

- "He who has health has hope. And he who has hope has everything." That ancient desert proverb is as relevant today as it was in the time of Christ. Your donation to the Hamilton Community Health Center can give health and hope to low-income families throughout our city.

- Robert Owens, the founder of Commercial-Kleen Janitorial Supplies, had a saying he always lived by: "If you treat your customers fairly, and go the extra mile, they'll treat you well, and your business will grow the extra mile." Those are words we've lived by ever since.

- William James, the famous philosopher, once observed that "the great use of life is to spend it for something that outlasts it." Setting up a living trust is a perfect example of that. Even after you're gone, your hard-earned wealth can continue to benefit your children, and your children's children, for years to come.

3. PAINT A SENSORY PICTURE THAT PUTS THE LISTENER IN THE SCENE

- Here's how we turn the world's best beef into the world's tastiest sandwich. We start with organic range-fed Angus beef from the high plains of Montana. We select the finest cuts, slow-steam them until they are tender enough to hand-pull, infuse them with our special barbecue sauce made from six rare tropical spices, then ladle a generous serving inside a warm toasted sesame-seed sourdough bun baked fresh that morning.

- The tension starts to melt away the moment you leave the city behind and enter the winding driveway through the pine forest. You are greeted at the door, given a private changing area and a freshly laundered white robe, and guided by your personal care specialist—first to the aromatic mud room, then to a series of cleansing herbal showers, and finally to a private massage table in a room.

- First, you and your daughter get to choose which kind of Teddy Bear you want to make. The brown one with button eyes and gentle smile? Or the pink one with the beret who's sticking his tongue out and laughing. Then, you get to choose his embroidered name and his outfit. For the next three hours, you'll love building a Teddy Bear together. But you're creating more than a Teddy Bear. You're creating the memory of a lifetime.

4. DRAMATIZE THE NEED

- Maybe you'll never lose your job, or get divorced, or run up huge medical bills and be unable to work. Maybe you'll never have to learn to walk again, or lose everything in a fire, or make a bad investment. But even if you never do, isn't it nice to know that you're covered financially, thanks to our new Catastrophe Insurance?

- It feels like you haven't eaten for days. It feels like you're in the hot dry desert miles from the nearest water. It feels like you haven't taken a break since you can't remember when. Well, when it feels like that, it sure feels good to take your full lunch hour and have a steak and a beer at McGonicles Chophouse and Brewery.

- Your avocado refrigerator hasn't been in style since 1972. Your linoleum tile has more chips in it than a potato factory. You adjust your stove with a pair of Vise-Grips®. And the breakfast nook actually has orange shag carpeting that belongs in the van you drove as a teenager. Well, perhaps it's time to get that home equity loan and remodel the kitchen.

5. LIST CUSTOMER CHOICES

- Grandpa wants something warm and comforting, like a burgundy steak with mashed potatoes and gravy? Aunt Tillie would like something light and fresh, like chilled gazpacho soup. The kids want a hot dog and fries and ice cream shakes. You're in the mood for a bowl of spaghetti carbonara. Where can you take everyone out to eat so they can all get what they want? Planet Food Court, that's where.

- We have fifteen hundred different shades of red paint. Everything from rose to fire engine red to salmon. We have twenty-three hundred shades of green. There's katydid green, moss, and celery green, to name but a few. We even have forty different shades of black paint. Bet you didn't know there were forty different shades of black! Well, who knows? You might like ebony better than jet black. You might like midnight black better than charcoal.

- So you get a book on gardening, but you get dirt on your carpet. Don't worry; we have a book on how to remove common household stains. In the course of removing the stain, you accidentally trip over the power cord of the carpet cleaner and pull out the wall socket. Don't worry; we have books on home repair, including electrical repair. Just as you finish fixing the wall socket, you realize that you might like to switch careers and become an electrician. Don't worry; we have books on how to switch careers.

6. LIST FEATURES AND BENEFITS

- We double-check all the tools before we rent them out. So you don't have the frustrating experience of taking the tool home only to find it doesn't work. We always include a free training and question-and-answer session when you rent your tool, so you know what you're doing and you don't hurt yourself. We have a 24-hour tool advisory service. So if you run into an unusual problem, you've got instant expert help.

- Our housepainters are all insured, so you don't have to worry about being liable if they fall off a ladder in your yard. They are all highly trained and experienced, which means that they know how to do the job right and do it fast. And they are all neat and clean, which means they don't leave you to dispose of their old paint cans; they take everything with them.

- All our beer is brewed fresh daily, which means the taste is robust, not flat. We use only the choicest hops, to assure you of the highest quality. We never heat or pasteurize our beer, because that destroys the flavor. And we use water directly from the natural spring beneath the brewery, so there is no artificial or chemical flavor—just pure, cold, wet beer.

7. DESCRIBE WHAT IS UNIQUE OR UNUSUAL OR EXTREME

■ The people who work for our housecleaning service are, frankly, a bit unusual. We only hire neatniks and clean freaks. The kind of people who obsess about how sanitary it is under the rim of the toilet. The kind of people who actually do take a white glove to the top shelf to make sure it has been properly dusted. Some might say they are obsessive-compulsive. We say, they are thoroughly committed to giving you a neat, clean house.

■ George Woods played on three winning Super Bowl teams. He was named MVP two of those times. When normal practice was done, he would head for the weight room to work an extra hour a night. George Woods brings excellence and commitment to everything he does. Which is why you should consider joining his new gym.

■ You can run over this titanium toolbox with your truck and you won't hurt it. You can shoot it with a shotgun and the pellets won't penetrate. You can chop the mailbox with an axe and all you'll get is a few dents. That's how strong and well made this toolbox is.

8. CONTRAST THE EXPERIENCE YOU PROVIDE WITH A TYPICAL CUSTOMER EXPERIENCE

■ If you're used to doctor clinics where you have to clear your throat to get the receptionist to notice you, where you sit and wait for nearly an hour until the doctor is ready to see you, and where there is no childcare to take the load off a mother who is not feeling so well, then you'll love Sunrise Clinic. We say hello the moment you walk through the door. A doctor sees you within 15 minutes or your visit is free. And we have a kids' playroom with a certified child-care professional always present.

- The average candy bar contains only 15% chocolate. The rest is basically sugar, wax, and preservatives. Which is why they can sit on the shelves at the grocery store for months at a time. But our chocolates all contain a minimum of 60% dark chocolate. They have no preservatives. Zero. Nada. Which is why you must eat them within two weeks of your purchase.

- The last time you tried to buy a car, did the salesman ask to speak to your husband? Did he call you "ma'am" or "missy"? When you explained you did not have a husband, did he try to hit on you? Did he then try to sell you a bunch of additional features you didn't want or need? And when you balked at the price, did he try to make a deal and then really pressure you to accept it? If so, then you'll love coming to our showroom. Half the salespeople are women. No one is on commission. And the price is the price, so no need to haggle.

Step 3. Prove Belief: 13 Ways to Prove That Listeners Can Believe You

Make sure you get the necessary legal permission to use names, testimonials, and certifications. Double-check your facts to make sure they are true—or you run the risk of permanently ruining your reputation and of inviting lawsuits for false advertising. Be particularly careful of superlative claims, like *always, never, guaranteed, promise, forever, permanently, unquestionably, absolutely, the best, better than, superior to, the only, exclusively,* etc.

1. PROVE CUSTOMER SATISFACTION

- 98% of our customers would recommend our services to a friend.
- 99.3% of our customers plan to purchase a car from us again.
- Over 90% of our customers this year are satisfied customers from previous years.

2. PROVE LEADERSHIP

- Our hospital was just certified by the American Hospital Association as one of the top hundred hospitals in the nation. Not in our city. In the nation.
- We've put more folks into their first home than any other Savings & Loan in Mount Carmel.

3. PROVIDE A CUSTOMER TESTIMONIAL

Be sure to get a signed talent release from the people whose names you mention in your commercial, authorizing you to use their names in any medium in perpetuity. You will need to pay them at least one dollar for the talent release to be valid. Check with the radio station or your lawyer for a sample form.

■ Mrs. A.K. Chesterson-Brawley wrote us a letter this month. "Dear Bob, I just wanted you to know what a wonderful employee you have in Kirsten R. She held onto my purchase so I could go back to the car and get my purse. Then she helped me carry my stuff to the car and load it in the trunk. She was very considerate."

■ Four times a year, like clockwork, Harold and Monica M. drive their Chevy S-10 pickup truck to our garage to get it fixed. What's unusual about that is that they live over one hundred miles away, in Macarthyburg. We asked them why they drive so far just to get their car fixed here. They said, "When you find a mechanic you can trust, you stick with them."

■ When 70-year-old Robert Omega finds something good, he sticks with it. He's been married to his wife, Charlene, for over 50 years. He's been living in the same house for over 45 years. And he's been getting his insurance coverage from Farm Owners General for over ... 51 years. His first agent was Arnold Fortuna, now a grandpa. He switched to Arnold Junior when Junior took over the business back in 1971. And he just switched to Arnold the third, or Trey, now that he's taken over this year.

4. PROVIDE AN EXPERT TESTIMONIAL

Be sure to get a signed talent release from the people whose names you mention in your commercial, authorizing you to use their names in any medium in perpetuity. You will need to pay them at least one dollar for the talent release to be valid. Check with the radio station or your lawyer for a sample form.

■ Nine out of ten dentists recommend using that toothpaste. Ten out of ten of our employees recommend you buy it from us, because you'll save 10%.

■ Cameron High School band leader Hannah Bell recommends that you purchase your student's instrument at Meier's MusicTown—and not just because we offer an automatic 10% discount to first-year band members, and an automatic 20% discount to second-year-plus members.

5. LIST CREDIBLE ENDORSEMENTS

Many endorsing organizations and certifiers have very specific rules about what you can and can't say in your advertising about their certification. You could lose your certification and risk a potential lawsuit if you violate even minor terms of the agreement. Check with the organization or your lawyer first.

■ Former Olympic Gold Medalist Aaron Carstin trains at the Pinehurst Gym.

■ Our diet products are approved by the American Heart Association as effective in reducing your chances of a heart attack.

■ Former five-time convicted burglar and felon "Rambo" Ronson says, quote, "Eventually I learned to walk away from any house with a "Protected by Booth Security" sign. I knew it would dramatically increase my chances of getting caught. In fact, four of the five times I was caught, it was a Booth Security silent alarm that was the problem."

6. LIST CERTIFICATIONS AND MEMBERSHIPS

- The majority of our mechanics are ASE-certified technicians.
- We're a member of the Better Business Bureau.
- Rama Forrest is a fully-certified Reiki Master and one of only three Americans certified in Japan.
- The Palladium Hotel has been awarded a five-star rating by Travelers Anonymous dot com.

7. OFFER A GUARANTEE OR MAKE-GOOD

Guarantees have legal ramifications. So make sure you can follow through on your promise and make sure a lawyer reviews your guarantee. You will also need to calculate the break-even point for your offer and estimate the chances you will at least cover your costs.

- If you're not absolutely satisfied with your Garden Grubber, return it within thirty days for a full refund, no questions asked.
- In the unlikely event that your computer has not been repaired properly, bring it in and we will repair it again for no charge.
- We're so certain you'll love getting a Sunday newspaper that, if you change your mind and cancel the service, we'll keep sending it to you free for another month.

8. PROVE QUALITY

- Our cabinets are made from the choicest cuts of lumber. We inspect every board for imperfections before we purchase it. We favor the hardest woods, like alder, ash, aspen, beech, and cherry. We have a special flattening and drying process that ensures the wood won't bend or warp after it has been joined. Essentially, we cure the wood for four months before we use it.

- Our "Death by Chocolate" chocolate truffles contain the highest percentage of cacao possible: 90% dark chocolate. Compare that with the 15% cacao in the average candy bar, and you'll see what we mean by world-class quality.

- These fleece jackets were tested in the Antarctic and are rated to keep you warm even when temperatures are up to, or rather down to, 70 below zero Fahrenheit.

9. OFFER A COMPELLING OR UNUSUAL STATISTIC, THE MORE PRECISE THE BETTER

- Most lawn mower engines are machined to within one one-hundredth of an inch. But our lawn mowers are machined to within one one-thousandth of an inch. That's hundreds of times smaller than the width of your eyelash.

- At Precision Accounting, we triple-check every tax return before it is submitted. We check it once by computer, once by our oversight committee, and once by an independent accountant. This ensures a 300% degree of confidence relative to the average tax return, and a 3000% degree of confidence relative to a standard accounting software program.

- If you are over age 65, you are 30% more likely to be killed by your own bathroom than by the combined causes of lightning, shark attacks, snakebite, and a plane crash. All it takes is one wrong fall and a head injury. So why not have Eldersafe Systems out to do a free safety analysis of your bathroom? Something as simple as a handrail in the bathtub could save your life.

10. INVITE SKEPTICS TO SEE FOR THEMSELVES

- Our new Rhinohide Truck Bed Liner is so tough you can beat it with a baseball bat and it will not crack or dent. The liner, that is. You may break the bat. If you try this test, we also suggest you remove the liner from your truck first. We have a supply of bats down at the dealership, so come on down and try it for yourself.

- If you think our promise is too good to be true, we invite you to visit our Web site at "I'm a skeptic dot com." We don't edit any of our customer feedback there. None. So what you read is the unvarnished truth. The good, the bad, and the ugly. The only person who can remove a comment is the customer who made it. See for yourself.

- Test-drive our new Gyrocycle on our specially designed track. Try to tip it over. You'll find that you can't, thanks to the built-in gyrowheel technology that keeps it upright no matter what. Our course includes jumps, and 45-degree banks, and sharp curves, and steep hills. Strap yourself into the new Gyrocycle and see for yourself. You can't tip one over.

11. STATE A GROWTH FACT

- Guess which Italian restaurant is the fastest-growing in America. Nope, it's not the name everybody knows. It's Luigivista's. For the last five years, the number of Luigivista's customers has grown an average of 200% a year. That's not just doubling. That's doubling the doubling. The reason is simple. Our food tastes so delizioso.

- Believe it or not, the number of indoor allergens has increased 40% over the last decade. The primary cause is the new materials being used in everything from sofa cushions to household cleaners. You can't see the out-gassing from these materials and you can't smell them. But they can cause severe allergic reactions such as rashes, difficulty breathing, headaches, and even sterility.

■ If you put one thousand dollars in a Local Bank money market CD today, and you leave it in for seven years at an average compound rate, your money will double. That's right: the magic of compound interest can turn one thousand dollars into two thousand dollars—and you don't have to report to work or lift a finger.

12. LIST YEARS OF EXPERIENCE

■ The ten acupuncture specialists at Lotus Blossom Center have a combined 200 years of professional acupuncture experience.

■ Mariposa Realty is now under the third generation of family management.

■ We've been installing underground pools in Clarion County since 1971.

13. PROVE AUTHENTIC MOTIVATION OR PASSION

■ When Dr. Carlson is not at his private practice here in Muhlenberg, he's most likely doing the same thing he likes to do, care for the sick, at the migrant labor camp down in Filene. Also, four times a year he travels with other physicians on a floating hospital to Third-World countries, where he helps treat everything from beriberi to vaccinations. In addition, 10% of the profits of his practice go to support the free clinic here in town.

■ When Susan was four, she made a mud pie. Then another. Then 40. The first thing she made in her EZ-Bake Oven was

… an apple pie. By the time she was 12, she could use a real oven and bake a real good peach pie with peaches fresh picked from her family's orchard. At 16, she won the county fair FFA blue ribbon prize for—you guessed it—the best pie, a rhubarb-blueberry compote with graham cracker crust. So it was only a matter of time before she started her own business, the appropriately named "Susan's Pies." You can go there today and have your choice of homemade—or rather "Susan-made"—pies.

- Homer at Homer's Family Photo Studio will do just about anything to make a young child laugh. Because he knows that one photo that captures that perfect moment of happiness will deserve a place on the wall for years to come, and that you can't go back years later and take it over. To make kids laugh, he's worn clown noses, stood on his head, quacked like a duck, and even hit himself in the face with a pie. Now that's the kind of guy who can make kids smile.

Step 4. Call to Action: 19 Ways to Ask Listeners to Do Something

1. REMEMBER YOUR NAME

- So remember our name: Blaine Hardware. Blaine. It rhymes with insane, as in our insanely low prices.

2. REMEMBER YOUR PHONE NUMBER

- Call 1-800-BUYAPIE. That's "1-800-Buy—B ... U ... Y ... —a— A ... —Pie—P ... I ... E ...."
- Get a pencil and paper now and write down our toll-free phone number. Ready? It's "one eight hundred buy a pie." That's "one eight hundred buy a pie."

3. REMEMBER YOUR WEB SITE

- For more information, visit our Web site at "www dot Christmas trees delivered dot com." That's "www dot Christmas trees delivered dot com."

4. REMEMBER YOUR NAME THE NEXT TIME A SITUATION ARISES

- So the next time the windshield on your car or truck cracks or breaks, remember to call Glassmasters at "five-five-five glass." That's "five-five-five," like the five fingers you can use to dial the phone, "glass, G ... L ... A ... S ... S...," like the glass we can install for you. Call "five-five-five glass" today.

5. CALL NOW FOR INFORMATION

- Operators are standing by 24/7, trained and ready to answer your questions, whether you are a customer or not. Call us toll-free at 1-800-555-5555. That's 1-800-555-5555. Call right now.

6. ORDER NOW

- Call now to order your own personalized mug at one-seven-six-five-five-five-five-four-four-four-four. That's one-seven-six-five- five-five-five-four-four-four-four. Or order online anytime at "www dot mega mug dot com." Get a free packet of hot chocolate with your shipment if you order online today at "www dot mega mug dot com."

7. ASK FOR THE ORDER

- Get your new Sleeperific king-sized bed right now and enjoy it tonight.

8. USE YOUR PRODUCT AND JUDGE FOR THEMSELVES

- We're so confident you will like the quality of our used cars that we are making this special offer. For only one hundred dollars, you can test-drive one of our used cars for seven days. If you don't like it, you don't have to buy it. The only catch is that you have to bring it back in the same condition as when you drove it off our lot, and you get only one offer like this from us for the rest of your life. So choose your car wisely.

9. ASK A FRIEND OR EXPERT TO RECOMMEND YOU

- Chances are, you already know someone who reads our newspaper every day. Ask them what they like about the Sunday Sentinel.

10. DON'T MISS A LIMITED OFFER

- Hurry! This three-for-two sale ends this Tuesday at 9:00 pm. Don't miss your chance to buy one pair of shoes and get two more at 50% off each.

11. VISIT OUR WEB SITE

■ To see the photos that we've taken of families and children, visit our Web site at "www dot picture your family dot com." That's "www dot picture your family dot com."

12. SEND FOR FREE NO-OBLIGATION INFORMATION

■ Call today and we'll send you a complete information kit that includes an evaluation of your talent, a brochure of course options and prices, and a free DVD with instructions on how to get started in an exciting new career as an artist. Order your free information kit within the next ten minutes, and we'll include a free Conté crayon and a sheet of museum-quality paper.

13. OFFER A SELF-TEST

■ Visit our Web site at "www dot insurance test dot com" and do a free insurance evaluation for yourself. The test takes only ten minutes, but it could save you thousands of dollars. The results are completely confidential and no salesperson will call on you.

14. ENTER TO WIN A PROMOTIONAL OFFER

■ Stop by this week and enter to win a free vacation for two to Cancun worth over $10,000! But hurry! The drawing is this Friday at 5 pm.

15. STOP BY OUR STORE

■ Drop in anytime and check out our showroom in the new Northtown Mall. We're right next to TGI Friday's. Children are welcome.

16. ATTEND A SPECIAL EVENT

■ Don't miss the grand opening of our Children's Gourmet Workshop. This weekend only, from noon to five on Saturday and Sunday, there'll be free five-course gourmet meal samples, cooking demonstrations, a live band, and free balloons for the children.

17. SUPPORT A GOOD CAUSE

■ This month, Huey's Canoe Outfitters will donate a portion of every purchase to Outward Bound, a nonprofit organization that helps troubled teens.

18. LIST ALL THE WAYS THE CUSTOMER CAN CONTACT YOU FOR MORE INFORMATION

Generally, you are better off selecting a primary means of contacting you and then repeating it. But if you need to list multiple means, here's one way to do it:

■ For more information, stop by your nearest Moneybank location, call our telebank at "one-two-three, four-five-six-six" or visit our Web site at "www dot telebank dot com."

19. STATE HOW CONVENIENT THE LOCATION OR HOURS ARE

■ The Best Little Restaurant in Texas is only a 15-minute drive from downtown Houston. Just head west on I-10 and take the Sugarland exit.

Step 5. Remember the Name: Eight Ways to Help Listeners Remember Your Name

1. REPEAT YOUR NAME

■ Stop by the Hair Artist Studio. That's the Hair Artist Studio, on Second Avenue.

2. USE A MEMORIZATION TRICK

■ Remember the name Barry Callen. That's "Barry," like straw-berry, and "Callen," like calendar.

3. TIE YOUR NAME TO YOUR CATEGORY DESCRIPTOR

See the "Slogans, Theme Lines, and Taglines" section of Chapter 2.

4. TIE YOUR NAME TO YOUR TAGLINE

See the "Slogans, Theme Lines, and Taglines" section of Chapter 2.

5. TIE YOUR NAME TO A SPECIFIC NEED OR CONDITION OR OCCASION

■ It's spring again, and that means the fire ant mounds are back. To get rid of them permanently before your children and pets start playing in the yard, call Besticide Service. When fire ants come back, don't use pesticides, call Besticide.

6. TIE YOUR NAME TO A REAL PERSON

■ Woods Lumber is not a made-up name. Jim Woods is a real guy who has lived here in Deerfield all his life. He started Woods Lumber over 20 years ago. So if you want a realtor who was born to be in the lumber business, call Jim Woods at Woods Lumber.

7. USE A JINGLE.

If you already have a short simple jingle that is fairly well-known, have the announcer sing it, even if badly.

- And folks, what I lack in ability I make up for in sincerity, when I say, ahem, (ANNOUNCER CLEARS THROAT AND SINGS JINGLE) "Forget the traffic and the fuss. Next time ride the city bus." (IF ANNOUNCER LAUGHS, LEAVE LAUGH IN)

8. TIE YOUR NAME TO A LOCATION OR LANDMARK

- Stop by Mannheim's newest furniture showroom, at the corner of State and Main, right across from the Coliseum.

Step 6. Write the Final Script

Assemble the parts.

RADIO COPY

CLIENT: New Breed Seed Corn

JOB NO.: XXXXXX

JOB NAME: Scientists or Farmers?

DATE: 10/06/07

REVISION: 3

PAGE 1 OF 1

ANNCR:

Farming has gotten so darned scientific that some days it's hard to know if you're a farmer or a scientist. So New Breed Seed Corn has devised this simple test.

If you know which metabolic pathway Zea Mays follows in C4-type photo-assimilate production, … you're a scientist.

If you know what has a straw walker, a cleaning fan, sieves, an auger, snapping rolls, and a corn head … and it isn't "a corn-headed auger walker?" … you're a farmer.

If you know both facts, you're probably a New Breed Seed Corn rep. Because New Breed Seed Corn is a unique marriage of science and farming. Our scientists grow new breeds of seeds, and our seed reps are mostly local farmers—who know which breeds work best on your particular farm.

So call your local New Breed Seed Corn rep at XXX-XXXX. That's XXX-XXXX.

New Breed Seed Corn makes the best feed corn.

Station-Produced Television Ad

A locally produced television commercial is less expensive than hiring an advertising agency, television production company, or film production company. You supply the basic information, or perhaps even a TV script, and the television station shoots and edits the commercial, provides the announcer and music, and makes the dubs that are sent to other TV stations.

Almost all TV commercials are 30 seconds long. You will need to make sure your TV script does not exceed 30 seconds or they will not be able to use it. A good rule of thumb is to write about 26 seconds of words or less. The more you can let the pictures tell the story, the better.

Use words that are short and easy to say. Write the way you speak, rather than writing to impress. Less is more. As on the radio, avoid lots of "S" words in a row and words with the letter "P."

There are many parallels between the phrases you write for your radio commercial and the phrases you write for your TV commercial. The only difference is that you can use fewer words because you can let the pictures tell more of the story.

Most TV commercials are 30 seconds long. Be sure you put a stopwatch to your finished script and read it out loud. TV stations won't run a commercial that goes over time by even a quarter second. To play it safe, write your script to take about 26 seconds to read for a 30-second commercial. This will give the announcer time to provide dramatic pauses and changes of pace for emphasis, and time to use a friendly, relaxing conversational style, instead of an irritating racing shout.

TV listeners are generally at home, not at the store. So it is important that they remember your name. It is generally a good idea to mention your product or company name at the very beginning, in the middle, and at the very end. Don't be afraid to repeat your name twice at the end.

TV viewers tune in for news and entertainment, not commercials. Make sure your commercial is either useful or enjoyable, and try to make it as unexpected as possible in order to get their attention. TV viewers are often doing other things while they are listening, like cooking or talking on the phone, so make sure your message is extremely clear and simple. Some repetition of main points can help.

The Five Steps in a Station-Produced TV Ad

Step 1. Get attention. Create a provocative opening to capture attention.

Step 2. Increase involvement. Paint a sensory picture or tell a story to emotionally hook the listeners.

Step 3. Prove belief. Prove that the listeners can believe you.

Step 4. Call to action. Ask the listeners to do something.

Step 5. Remember the name. Help the listeners remember your name.

Time-Saving Tip: You can use almost the exact same information for both your locally produced TV script and your live-read radio script: same opening, interest, proof, call to action, and name. Doing so saves time and helps reinforce your message and make it more memorable. This is "integrated marketing communications" and it helps build "brand equity" for a higher long-term return on your communications investment.

However, you will need to reduce the number of words in your 60-second radio script by about 60 to 70% in order to fit

---

them into your 30-second TV spot. To see how this is done, compare and contrast the radio and TV examples in this book that use similar creative approaches.

While you communicate the same core message in both media, you can use visuals to communicate most of the information in your TV commercial. People generally expect TV commercials to be briefer and more entertaining.

Dos and Don'ts

- Do use a two-column script with the visuals described on the left and the words on the right.

- Do type your script and double-check it for factual errors. Triple-check the contact information.

- Do favor visual communication over verbal. Instead of describing how great a meal tastes, show it beautifully presented, steaming hot, with melting butter, and vibrant colors. A picture is worth a thousand words in television.

- Do use "supers" to reinforce key information. Supers are the words typed on the screen that are superimposed over the screen image. For example, when you say, "Call 1-800-FIX-TOYS," simultaneously super:

Call 1-800-FIX-TOYS.
(1-800-349-8697)

- Do make sure your supers and key information are within the safe-action area. That is, far enough from the edge of the screen so that they will be clearly visible and not cut off on any television set, regardless of shape and model.

- Don't exaggerate or make false claims of superiority or you will open yourself up to potential lawsuits and increase negative word of mouth among customers.

- Don't make superlative claims like *always, never, guaranteed, promise, forever, permanently, unquestionably, absolutely, the best, better than, superior to, the only, exclusively*, etc. unless you can prove them.

- Do make sure your script takes less than 30 seconds to read at a normal pace. Aim for 26 seconds. Use a stopwatch.

- Do make your opening surprising, unexpected, newsworthy, entertaining, or useful.

- Don't use circus promotion language like *amazing, greatest*, or *unbelievable* or general or abstract words like *quality, convenience, advanced, partnership*, and *solutions*.

- Do mention your company name two to three times. The best times are at the beginning, in the middle, and at the end.

- Do repeat your phone number at least twice. This will give viewers time to write it down.

- Do make one main point per commercial—and then prove it.

- Don't make your commercial a long list of claims. People won't remember them.

- Do make sure you include one simple call to action.

- Don't imitate what your competitors are doing, especially your largest competitors, or people will confuse your commercials for theirs. Then you've wasted your money.

- Don't write tongue-twisters or use lots of "S" words in a row. They are hard to say.

- Don't use lots of words that begin with "P." They tend to make a popping sound.

- Do write to be clear, rather than to be clever. Say something worth hearing.

■ Do make sure you are prepared to handle a sudden increase in store visits or call volume.

Creative Tip: As with radio ads, choose a single perspective—"you" or "we" or "they"—and stick with your choice. See examples on page 92.

Step 1. Get Attention: 16 Ways to Create a Provocative Opening

1. ANNOUNCE NEWS

- Like Rangemaster appliances? We've just been chosen as the exclusive area distributor.
- Our new locator technology can find your lost or stolen cell phone.
- Announcing a breakthrough in home water treatment.

2. REFER TO A CURRENT EVENT

- Get all your Christmas shopping done in July!
- School's almost out, and it's time to check and see if you're almost out of suntan lotion.
- If you're celebrating a birthday this month, come to our restaurant for a free cake.

3. REFER TO THE LOCAL AREA

- The Maxwell Street Food Fair will feature hundreds of booths and cuisines.
- Is there anything more beautiful than the Blue Ridge Parkway in the fall?
- Memorial High School will be holding a car wash at Zowiki's Texaco this Saturday.

4. REFER TO THE WEATHER

- Put down some MiraGro Fertilizer before the next big rain.
- After three weeks of drought, it's time to invest in a lawn sprinkler system.
- Spring is just around the corner. Have you got all your garden supplies?

5. CREATE URGENCY

- We've only got 300 pairs of shoes left—and when they're gone, they're gone.
- The concert hall is almost filled for the Friday night concert, but if you call now, you can reserve a seat.
- Don't miss this once-in-a-lifetime offer.

6. USE A SURPRISING FACT

- Here are three things your spouse will never tell you, even if you ask.
- More Americans die from bathroom falls than from nuclear power.
- Three years from now, nine out of ten new businesses will be out of business.

7. OFFER A PROMOTION

- 10% of all sales will be donated to New Orleans hurricane relief.
- Anyone under 18 will get in free this weekend.
- This weekend, everything in our store is 50% off.

8. FLAG YOUR CUSTOMER

- Join our Seniors Discount Club. The older you are, the more benefits you earn.
- Attention, boating enthusiasts!
- Got a critter you can't seem to get rid of? We can handle it.

9. CONTRADICT A BELIEF

- Think all used car salesmen are liars? Think again.
- We're like no delivery service you've ever seen.
- Who says you have to be rich to get the best hotel suite?

10. STATE A BENEFIT

- We offer free home delivery with every purchase over $100.
- College graduates earn over a million dollars more in their lifetime.
- Cut your heating bills 25% a year.

11. TELL HOW YOU ARE UNIQUE

Make sure you can prove your unique claim.

- We carry one of the area's largest selections of bedroom and bath tiles.
- You don't drive to our storage facility. We drop off a container at your home.
- We were voted "Best Hamburger in the City" in the last Metro Magazine readers poll.

12. STATE A PROBLEM TO SOLVE

- Face it. Your career is going nowhere fast.
- Take a good honest look at your house. Does it need repainting?
- Need money fast? If you've got a job, you've got a loan.

13. ASK A QUESTION

- Where can you go to find the latest in quilting supplies?
- Who do more Chicagoans turn to when they need to sell their homes?
- Tired of putting up with windows that won't open?

14. USE AN UNUSUAL WORD

- Hellfire. That's right. Our chili is so hot, we named it Hellfire Chili.
- If there was one word to describe our bike courier service, it would be "¡Ándale!"

- When you see our collection of '50s retro clothing, you'll say "Neato. Keeno. Spiffy."

15. USE YOUR CATEGORY DESCRIPTOR

This helps integrate your communications for a higher return on investment. To create a better business category descriptor, see the "Slogans, Theme Lines, and Taglines" section of Chapter 2, pages 13–19.

- We fix broken windshields. Anytime. Anywhere.
- We're more than a community college. We're your ticket to a better career.
- For secretaries, receptionists, and administrative assistants, call QuickTemp.

16. USE YOUR PRINT AD HEADLINE

This helps integrate your communications for a higher return on investment. To create a better headline, see the "Headlines" section of Chapter 2, pages 21–27.

Step 2. Increase Involvement: Eight Ways to Emotionally Hook Viewers

Now that you've gotten your viewers' attention, you want to interest them in finding out more about your story. You want to get them emotionally engaged. The best way to do this is to use your words to trigger their imagination. Help them see what you are saying in their mind's eye or on the screen. This is the place for drama, entertainment, sensory detail, experiences, and stories.

1. TELL A STORY

- One hour after a tornado completely destroyed their home, Bob and Carol Owens had a hotel room, a thermos of hot coffee, and a check for $200,000, courtesy of their insurance agent, Mary Quintanos.
- Jamal Washington started working on engines when he was seven. He never stopped. Today he owns the area's first sports car repair service: Jamar's SportCar Shop.
- University Community College helped Henrietta earn her high-school diploma, get college scholarships, and earn a college degree—despite her wheelchair. Today she is a supervisor who earns a six-figure income in a state government job.

2. QUOTE A PERSON

- "The greatest wealth is health." —Virgil
- They say nothing is certain but death and taxes. We can help with the taxes part. We're Rogerstein and Feldbaum, Certified Public Accounts.
- "Out, damned spot! Out, I say!" Obviously Lady Macbeth

didn't know about Hydroclean, the new superpowered stain remover available at Forborn Drugstores.

3. PAINT A SENSORY PICTURE THAT PUTS THE LISTENER IN THE SCENE

- To turn the world's best beef into the world's tastiest sandwich, we start with organic Montana range-fed Angus, slow-steam the finest cuts, infuse the beef with our tropical barbecue sauce, and ladle it on a fresh-baked sourdough bun.

- Leave your city cares behind. Smell the pine forest. Don a freshly laundered white robe. Relax as your personal care specialist treats you to an aromatic mud bath, cleansing herbal showers, and a private massage.

- Together you choose the Teddy Bear you want to make, right down to his name and outfit. For the next three hours you don't just create a Teddy Bear—you create the memory of a lifetime.

4. DRAMATIZE THE NEED

- Should you ever have significant financial losses or be unable to work or walk, you'll find some comfort in knowing that you're covered financially by our new Catastrophe Insurance.

- Hungry? Thirsty? Need a break? Have a steak and a beer for lunch today at McGonicles Chophouse and Brewery.

- Tired of the avocado refrigerator and shag carpeting from the '70s? Tired of the chipped linoleum floor and the broken stove? Then it's time to remodel your kitchen with a home equity loan from us.

5. LIST CUSTOMER CHOICES

- Our menu has everything from steaks and gazpacho soup and spaghetti carbonara for the adults to hot dogs, fries, and ice cream for the kids. With over 200 menu items, everyone can get what they want at Planet Food Court.

- We have fifteen hundred different shades of red paint, forty different shades of black paint, and five thousand color choices altogether. Whatever your favorite color is, we've probably got it.

- We have books on everything from how to get rid of common household stains to how to get rid of your husband. Over 10,000 books in all.

6. LIST FEATURES AND BENEFITS

- You know your tool will work because we've double-checked it. You know how to use it because we've trained you. And for unusual problems, you know you can call our experts 24/7.

- All our housepainters are insured, so you don't have to worry about accidents. All are trained and experienced, so they work fast. And all are neat and clean, so you don't have to clean up after them.

- All our beer is brewed fresh daily, and never heated or pasteurized, for full flavor. Natural spring water from beneath the brewery is free of any chemical taste. The result: just pure, cold, wet beer.

7. DESCRIBE WHAT IS UNIQUE OR UNUSUAL OR EXTREME

- Our housecleaning service hires only neatniks and clean freaks. Some might say they are obsessive-compulsive. We say, they are thoroughly committed to giving you a neat, clean house.

- Former MVP George Woods played on three winning Super Bowl teams. Every night after practice he put an extra hour in the weight room. George Woods brings the same excellence and commitment to his new gym.

- You can run over this new titanium toolbox with your truck, shoot it with a shotgun, or chop it with an axe, but you can't hurt it. That's how strong and well made it is.

8. CONTRAST THE EXPERIENCE YOU PROVIDE WITH A TYPICAL CUSTOMER EXPERIENCE

- If you're used to being ignored and held up at the doctor's office, you'll love Sunrise Clinic. You see a doctor within 15 minutes or your visit is free. And your kids will love our playroom.

- The average candy bar contains only 15% chocolate. But our chocolates all contain a minimum of 60% dark chocolate. They have no preservatives. Zero. Nada. Which is why you must eat them within two weeks of your purchase.

- Our salespeople will not ask to speak to your husband, will not call you "ma'am" or "missy," and will not try to hit on you or sell you a bunch of additional features you didn't want or need. Half our salespeople are women. No one is on commission. And the price is the price, so no need to haggle.

Step 3. Prove Belief: 13 Ways to Prove That Viewers Can Believe You

Make sure you get the necessary legal permission to use names, testimonials, and certifications. Double-check your facts to make sure they are true or you run the risk of permanently ruining your reputation and of inviting lawsuits for false advertising. Be particularly careful of superlative claims like *always, never, guaranteed, promise, forever, permanently, unquestionably, absolutely, the best, better than, superior to, the only, exclusively*, etc.

1. PROVE CUSTOMER SATISFACTION

- Every day our restaurant gets at least ten employees ordering carry-out …, employees who work for other restaurants but like our pizza better.
- Last year, 90% of our growth came from previous clients who wanted us to do more for them.
- We process over 10,000 orders a year, but we receive fewer than ten customer complaints a year.

2. PROVE LEADERSHIP

- In a recent Consumer Publication, our microwaves were rated highest in durability and customer satisfaction.
- Every week, the largest karaoke crowds are to be found at The Harmony Pub.
- The readers of Downtown Magazine rated our bed-and-breakfast as number one for three years in a row.

3. PROVIDE A CUSTOMER TESTIMONIAL

Be sure to get a signed talent release from the people whose names you mention in your commercial, authorizing you to use their names in any medium in perpetuity. You will need to pay them at least one dollar for the talent release to be valid. Check with the radio station or your lawyer for a sample form.

- According to a letter from Mrs. A.K. Chesterson-Brawley, one of our employees, Kirsten R., held onto her purchase so she could find her purse. Then she helped Mrs. Chesterson-Brawley carry her purchase to the car and load it into the trunk.

- Four times a year, like clockwork, Harold and Monica M. drive their Chevy S-10 pickup truck over one hundred miles to get their car fixed at our garage. They said they do it because "When you find a mechanic you can trust, you stick with him."

- 70-year-old Robert Omega has been getting his insurance coverage from Farm Owners General for over ... 51 years. His first agent was Arnold Fortuna, his second agent was Arnold Junior, and his current agent is Arnold the third, or Trey.

4. PROVIDE AN EXPERT TESTIMONIAL

Be sure to get a signed talent release from the people whose names you mention in your commercial, authorizing you to use their names in any medium in perpetuity. You will need to pay them at least one dollar for the talent release to be valid. Check with the radio station or your lawyer for a sample form.

- Nine out of ten dentists recommend using that toothpaste. Ten out of ten of our employees recommend you buy it from us, because you'll save 10%.

- Cameron High School band leader Hannah Bell recommends that you purchase your student's instrument at Meier's MusicTown—and not just because we offer an automatic 10% discount to first-year band members, and an automatic 20% discount to second-year-plus members.

5. LIST CREDIBLE ENDORSEMENTS

Many endorsing organizations and certifiers have very specific rules about what you can and can't say in your advertising about their certification. You could lose your certification and risk a potential lawsuit if you violate even minor terms of the agreement. Check with the organization or your lawyer first.

- Former Olympic Gold Medalist Aaron Carstin trains at the Pinehurst Gym.
- Our diet products are approved by the American Heart Association as effective in reducing your chances of a heart attack.
- Four of the five times that convicted house burglar "Rambo" Ronson was caught, it was a Booth Security silent alarm that caught him. Now he won't go anywhere near a home with a Booth Security sign.

6. LIST CERTIFICATIONS AND MEMBERSHIPS

- The majority of our mechanics are ASE-certified technicians.
- We're a member of the Better Business Bureau.
- Rama Forrest is a fully certified Reiki Master and one of only three Americans certified in Japan.
- The Palladium Hotel has been awarded a five-star rating by Travelers Anonymous dot com.

7. OFFER A GUARANTEE OR MAKE-GOOD

Guarantees have legal ramifications. So make sure you can follow through on your promise and make sure a lawyer reviews your guarantee. You will also need to calculate the break-even point for your offer and estimate the chances you will at least cover your costs.

- If you're not absolutely satisfied with your Garden Grubber, return it within 30 days for a full refund, no questions asked.
- In the unlikely event that your computer has not been repaired properly, bring it in and we will repair it again for no charge.
- We're so certain you'll love getting a Sunday newspaper that, if you change your mind and cancel the service, we'll keep sending it to you free for another month.

8. PROVE QUALITY

- Our cabinets are made from the choicest cuts of lumber and the hardest woods. We inspect every piece and we use a special flattening and drying process to prevent bending and warping.
- Our "Death by Chocolate" chocolate truffles contain the highest percentage of cacao possible: 90% dark chocolate. Compare that with the 15% cacao in the average candy bar and you'll see what we mean by world-class quality.
- These fleece jackets were tested in the Antarctic and are rated to keep you warm even when temperatures are up to, or rather down to, 70 below zero Fahrenheit.

9. OFFER A COMPELLING OR UNUSUAL STATISTIC, THE MORE PRECISE THE BETTER

- Most lawn mower engines are machined to within one

one-hundredth of an inch. But our lawn mowers are machined to within one one-thousandth of an inch.

- At Precision Accounting, we triple-check every tax return by computer, by committee, and by independent auditor before it is submitted. This ensures a 300% degree of confidence relative to the average tax return.

- If you are over age 65, you are 30% more likely to be killed by your own bathroom than by the combined causes of lightning, shark attacks, snakebite, and a plane crash. Eldersafe Systems can do a free safety analysis of your bathroom that could save your life.

10. INVITE SKEPTICS TO SEE FOR THEMSELVES

- You can beat our new Rhinohide Truck Bed Liner with a baseball bat and it will not crack or dent. We have a supply of bats down at the dealership. Come and try it for yourself.

- If you think our promise is too good to be true, we invite you to visit our Web site at I'm a skeptic dot com. We don't edit any of our customer feedback there. None.

- Test-drive our new Gyrocycle on our specially designed track. Try to tip it over. You'll find that you can't, thanks to the built-in gyrowheel technology that keeps it upright no matter what.

11. STATE A GROWTH FACT

- Guess which Italian restaurant is the fastest growing in America. Nope, it's not the name everybody knows. It's Luigivista's. We're growing 200% a year, because our food tastes so delizioso.

- Believe it or not, the number of indoor allergens has increased 40% over the last decade. The primary cause is the new materials being used in everything from sofa cushions to household cleaners.

- If you put one thousand dollars in a Local Bank money market CD today, and you leave it in for seven years at an average compound rate, your money will double. What are you waiting for?

12. LIST YEARS OF EXPERIENCE

- The ten acupuncture specialists at Lotus Blossom Center have a combined 200 years of professional acupuncture experience.
- Mariposa Realty is now under the third generation of family management.
- We've been installing underground pools in Clarion County since 1971.

13. PROVE AUTHENTIC MOTIVATION OR PASSION

- When Dr. Carlson is not at his private practice here in Muhlenberg, he's most likely volunteering to care for the sick at a migrant labor camp or on a floating hospital. 10% of the profits of his practice go to support the free clinic here in town.
- The first thing Susan made in her EZ-Bake Oven was … an apple pie. At 16, she won the county fair FFA blue ribbon prize for her pie. So it was only a matter of time before she started her own business, the appropriately named "Susan's Pies."
- Homer at Homer's Family Photo Studio will do just about anything to make a young child laugh. He's worn clown noses, stood on his head, quacked like a duck, and even hit himself in the face with a pie. Now that's the kind of guy who can make kids smile.

Step 4. Call to Action: 18 Ways to Ask Viewers to Do Something

1. REMEMBER YOUR NAME

- So remember our name: Rollity Realty. Rollity. It rhymes with "quality."

2. REMEMBER YOUR PHONE NUMBER

- Call 1-800-EATCORN. That's "1-800- … E … A … T … C … O … R … N."
- Write down this number. Call 1-800-EATCORN. Dial it just like you spell it.

3. REMEMBER YOUR WEB SITE

- For more information, visit our Web site at "www dot shoes are better than sex dot com." That's "www dot shoes are better than sex dot com."

4. REMEMBER YOUR NAME THE NEXT TIME A SITUATION ARISES

- So the next time the windshield on your car or truck cracks or breaks, remember to call Glassmasters at "five-five-five glass." That's "five-five-five," like the five fingers you can use to dial the phone, "glass, G … L … A … S … S…," like the glass we can install for you. Call "five-five-five glass" today.

5. CALL NOW FOR INFORMATION

- Operators are standing by 24/7. Call us toll-free at 1-800-555-5555. That's 1-800-555-5555. Call right now.

6. ORDER NOW

- Call now to order your own personalized mug at 1-555-5555. That's 1-555-5555. Get a free packet of hot chocolate with your shipment if you order online today at "www dot mega mug dot com."

7. ASK FOR THE ORDER

- Get your new washer/dryer combo right now and use it tonight.

8. USE YOUR PRODUCT AND JUDGE FOR THEMSELVES

- For only one hundred dollars, you can test-drive one of our used cars for seven days. If you don't like it, you don't have to buy it.

9. ASK A FRIEND OR EXPERT TO RECOMMEND YOU

- Chances are, you already know someone who reads our newspaper every day. Ask them what they like about the Sunday Sentinel.

10. DON'T MISS A LIMITED OFFER

- Hurry! This three-for-two sale ends this Tuesday at 9:00 pm. Don't miss your chance to buy one pair of shoes and get two more at 50% off each.

11. VISIT OUR WEB SITE

- To see the photos that we've taken of families and children, visit our Web site at "www dot picture your family dot com." That's "www dot picture your family dot com."

12. SEND FOR FREE NO-OBLIGATION INFORMATION

- Call today and we'll send you a complete information kit that includes a free DVD on how to get started in an exciting new career as an artist. Order your free information kit within the next ten minutes, and we'll include a free Conté crayon and a sheet of museum-quality paper.

13. OFFER A SELF-TEST

- Visit our Web site at "www dot insurance test dot com" and do a free insurance evaluation for yourself. The test takes only ten minutes, but it could save you thousands of dollars. The results are completely confidential and no salesperson will call on you.

14. ENTER TO WIN A PROMOTIONAL OFFER

- Stop by this week and enter to win a free vacation for two to Cancun worth over $10,000! But hurry! The drawing is this Friday at 5 pm.

15. STOP BY OUR STORE

- Drop in anytime and check out our showroom in the new Northtown Mall. We're right next to TGI Friday's. Children are welcome.

16. ATTEND A SPECIAL EVENT

- Don't miss the grand opening of our Children's Gourmet Workshop. This weekend only, from noon to five on Saturday and Sunday, there'll be free five-course gourmet meal samples, cooking demonstrations, a live band, and free balloons for the children.

17. SUPPORT A GOOD CAUSE

- This month, Huey's Canoe Outfitters will donate a portion of every purchase to Outward Bound, a nonprofit organization that helps troubled teens.

18. STATE HOW CONVENIENT THE LOCATION OR HOURS ARE

- The Best Little Restaurant in Texas is only a 15-minute drive from downtown Houston. Just head west on I-10 and take the Sugarland exit.

Step 5. Remember the Name: Five Ways to Help Viewers Remember Your Name

1. REPEAT YOUR NAME

- Stop by the Hair Artist Studio. That's the Hair Artist Studio, on Second Avenue.

2. USE A MEMORIZATION TRICK

- Remember the name Barry Callen. That's "Barry," like strawberry, and "Callen," like calendar.

3. TIE YOUR NAME TO A SPECIFIC NEED OR CONDITION OR OCCASION

- It's spring again, and that means the fire ant mounds are back. To get rid of them permanently before your children and pets start playing in the yard, call Besticide Service. When fire ants come back, don't use pesticides, call Besticide.

4. TIE YOUR NAME TO A REAL PERSON

- Woods Lumber is not a made-up name. Jim Woods is a real guy who has lived here in Deerfield all his life. He started Woods Lumber over 20 years ago. So if you want a realtor who was born to be in the lumber business, call Jim Woods at Woods Lumber.

5. TIE YOUR NAME TO A LOCATION OR LANDMARK

- Stop by Mannheim's newest furniture showroom at the corner of State and Main, right across from the coliseum.

Step 6. Write the Script

Assemble the parts into a two-column script.

:30 TELEVISION COPY

CLIENT: Corprov (Corporate Improv)	JOB NO.: XXXXXX
JOB NAME: Playing Games	DATE: 9/23/07
REVISION: 2	PAGE 1 OF 1

VIDEO	AUDIO
1) OPEN ON A GROUP OF ADULT EMPLOYEES PLAYING ZIP ZAP ZOP GAME AND LAUGHING	ANNCR (VO): Corprov uses improv comedy games to train corporate employees to be more creative, better listeners, and better partners.
2) CUT TO VARIOUS SHOTS OF EMPLOYEES PLAYING GAMES AND LAUGHING	Anyone who can walk and talk can play improv games. You don't have to be funny at all.
3) CUT TO BARRY IN THE CENTER OF A CIRCLE OF PEOPLE GIVING INSTRUCTIONS	We bring over 14 years of improv experience teaching well-known corpora-tions.
4) CUT TO CLOSEUP OF BARRY CALLEN SMILING	Contact Corprov founder, Barry Callen, ...

5) SUPER: Corprov Logo	... at 608 347 8396. That's Corprov, Corporate Improv corporate improv, at 608 347 8396. That's 608 347 8396.

CREATIVE TIP: Use standard abbreviations to provide directions in your TV script. You don't have to use these abbreviations, but it helps.

VIDEO:

The image. Anything in the left column of the script is visual. It is what gets shot with the camera. Or it is the logos and words that are superimposed (supered) over the image. It can be film, video, photos, or illustrations.

AUDIO:

The sound. Anything in the right column of the script is sound. It can be an announcer, someone speaking on camera, a sound effect, or music.

ANNCR:

Announcer. This is a person who reads the script. The announcer can be recorded either on camera (OC) or as a voice-over (VO).

VO:

Voice-over. Usually the announcer does a voice-over, meaning that he or she does not appear on camera. Voice-overs are usually recorded separately in a studio, for better audio quality.

OC:

On camera. This means the individual who is speaking is being recorded on camera, instead of separately in a studio. It means that his or her words and mouth must be in sync. It is more expensive to change an OC recording than a VO recording, because you have to reshoot the video. A typical way of indicating OC in a script is to name the actor, followed by OC. For example:

FATHER (OC): My daughter loves this toy.

DAUGHTER (OC) (TO FATHER): Thanks, Dad!

SUPER:

Superimposed over the screen image. Words and numbers are often "supered" for emphasis. Typically this includes key points, logos, slogans, and legal type.

BUILDING SUPER:

A super in which each line is added one at a time. It builds.

BUILDING SUPER:

LOGO (and then)

SLOGAN: We make it work.

CUT TO:

This indicates that an image or scene has ended and a new image or scene has begun. A hard cut is when there is no transition, a soft cut is when the transition takes a bit longer, and a dissolve is when the two images overlap briefly. A standard cut works for most locally produced TV commercials. Your TV production company editor can advise you on the best cuts to use.

Words continue across a visual cut. For example, an

announcer continues talking while the video image changes. See the script above for use.

SFX:

Sound effects. Sometimes your TV production partner has some sound effects that can be dropped into your audio track for emphasis. For example, the sound of a car horn honking would be indicated this way:

SFX (CAR HORN HONKING):

MUSIC:

Music comes in two forms, either a music bed, which flows beneath the words being spoken to create a feeling in the viewer, or a jingle, a catchy tune with catchy words intended to stick in your memory. Most jingles are used repeatedly in order to drive them into your memory. There are two kinds of music beds: original music, created specifically for your commercial by a composer and a music production house, or needledrop or prerecorded music. Either way, make absolutely sure you own the full rights to use the music or you could be hit with an expensive lawsuit.

Music is typically indicated like this:

MUSIC (UNDER AND THROUGHOUT):

This means the music floats beneath the surface of the commercial for the duration of the TV spot, like a soundtrack.

Chapter 5
Tactics for Postcards, Letters, and Sell Sheets

Postcards

Your readers get a huge pile of mail everyday that they or their secretaries glance at for half a second and then decide to toss or keep. To not get tossed, your piece must get to the point right away with something unexpected or useful. So few people receive postcards from friends these days that most postcards are automatically assumed to be junk mail. The exceptions are postcards that are handwritten or hand-signed, use a first-class stamp, or make a personal reference (computer personalized).

On the plus side, postcards are the least expensive form of snail mail, so you can print and send them in greater number. Postcards can communicate simple information quickly. And postcards are perfect when you have something very simple to communicate, particularly news or announcements. For example, a postcard is a good way to announce a special event or limited promotion. A postcard may seem simple but it has 13 components:

Front Side

1. Main visual
2. Headline
3. Subhead
4. Logo
5. Slogan

Back Side

6. Mailing indicia or stamp
7. Mailing address label
8. Headline
9. Subhead
10. Body copy
11. Call to action
12. Logo or name
13. Slogan

Three things determine the effectiveness of your mailing, in order of importance:

1. The quality of your mailing list—are they names of previous buyers or total strangers? Is the information up to date or outdated?
2. The quality and timing of your offer—is it new and exciting? Is it different from what's expected? Are customers ready to buy?
3. The quality of the creative execution—is it clear and well written? Does the design get attention? Is it easy to read?

Dos and Don'ts

- Do make sure you have an excellent mailing list (previous customers, previous interest, updated and current information).

- Do use an arresting, attention-getting visual.
- Do have a compelling offer that is both appealing and unexpected.
- Do consider the timing of your mailing. First, check with the Postal Service for an estimate of how long it will take them to deliver your mailing. (This will depend on the size and the range of geographic locations.) Second, mail when customers are ready to buy or beginning to think about what to buy. For example, most Christmas presents are purchased in December. Mailing in February would produce dramatically worse results.
- Do use the same headline and subhead on the front and the back of the card. There's a 50/50 chance the recipient will see the back of your postcard first.
- Do look for opportunities to personalize your postcard: handwritten or hand-signed, first-class stamp, or computer-personalized words.
- Do use powerful selling words like *free*, *new*, *now*, *introducing*, and *save*.
- Do avoid general or abstract words like *quality*, *convenience*, *advanced*, *partnership*, and *solutions*.
- Don't reverse out the type in your body copy (white letters on a black background). It can reduce readability by as much as 60%.
- Do make one main point per postcard—and then prove it.
- Don't make your ad a long list of claims.
- Do make sure you include a call to action. It can increase results by as much as 20%.
- Don't imitate what your competitors are doing. Do stand out.
- Do check with the Postal Service regarding approved sizes,

shapes, label, and postage requirements before you print your postcards.

■ Do use split-run testing. (Two versions, different in one major aspect and the contact number. You then measure the difference in results.) Then keep trying to beat your control postcard with new lists, new offers, and new creative approaches.

> **Time-Saving Tip:** You can use almost the same information for your postcard as for your print ads and brochure: same visuals, same headline, etc. Again, this repetition saves you time, helps reinforce your message and make it more memorable, and builds "brand equity."
>
> While you communicate the same core message in all three media, you provide the least explanation in your postcards. People generally expect postcards to get to the point quickly.

Nine Steps to Creating a Postcard

To create your postcard, create the eight pieces of your postcard and then put them all together.

Step 1. Select a photo or illustration.

Here are some classic subjects for your photo or illustration:

■ Your product or service

■ A person using your product or service (get a signed talent release)

■ The benefit of your product or service

■ The problem your product or service solves

■ A satisfied customer (get a signed talent release)

■ A map showing your location

■ A picture of your store or facility

- A dramatic demonstration of your product or service
- A cutaway view of the inside of your product
- A special event
- A celebrity at the special event (get a signed talent release)
- An invitation
- A prize you can win at a contest (There are many legal restrictions in running contests. Check with your lawyer first.)

Step 2. Create a headline.

The headline should state your single most important point. Use the creative approaches to writing a headline presented in Chapter 2, pages 21–27. You should put your headline on the front and on the back of your postcard, because there is a 50/50 chance the recipient reader will see the back first.

Step 3. Create a subhead.

The subhead should state your second-most important point. Use the creative approaches to writing a subhead presented in Chapter 2, page 28. Make sure the headline and subhead don't duplicate each other. Use type size and placement to make sure the headline is read first and the subhead is read second. Put your subhead on the front and on the back of your postcard.

Step 4. Write body copy.

You will need to limit your words because of space—50 to 100 words at most. Your first paragraph should amplify or prove the point you are making in the headline or subhead. Keep it short. Hit the highlights. In the middle, you should provide intriguing or unexpected details. Then end with a call to action.

- Use the 11 creative approaches to writing a first paragraph for a print ad on page 37.
- Use the 11 creative approaches to writing a first paragraph

for a brochure on pages 52–57.

- Use the 4 creative approaches to writing body copy for a print ad on pages 43–44.
- Use the 4 creative approaches to writing body copy for a brochure on pages 58–60.

Step 5. Create a call to action.

Use the creative approaches in Chapter 2, pages 30 31 to create a better call to action.

Step 6. Place your name or logo.

For a better name, use the creative approaches presented in Chapter 2, pages 7–11. In general, you should place your logo in the lower right of your ad or in the bottom at the center.

Step 7. Add your slogan.

For a better slogan, see the creative approaches presented in Chapter 2, pages 13–19. Your slogan should generally run either just below your logo or at the bottom of your ad.

Step 8. Add indicia (for mailing in bulk).

You will need an indicia on the back panel of your postcard that contains mailing information. As explained earlier, an indicia is a rectangle that contains postal information (usually a special number or bar code) necessary to send your postcard through the mail at a bulk rate (usually a standard rate or third-class rate). To qualify for this special rate, you generally must mail at least 500 identical pieces at a time. You must get your indicia from the Postal Service. The Postal Service is very particular about what information the indicia must contain and how the indicia and mailing panel should be laid out. Check with the Postal Service regarding the size and shape and paper stock and weight of your postcard. Also show them your layout before you get your postcard printed, particularly the indicia and the mailing label area.

Step 9. Assemble all the pieces into a postcard.

Use type size, boldness, color, and placement to make sure there is a clear hierarchy of dominance: a most important thing, a second-most important thing, and so forth. This will help guide the readers' eyes to the most important things on your postcard. Use bullets and short phrases that are easy to scan.

Three Creative Approaches to Writing Postcard Body Copy

1. TELL THE RECIPIENTS WHY YOU ARE MAILING TO THEM SPECIFICALLY

- Planning to attend the Annual Professional Conference in Las Vegas in July? Stop by our booth.
- Our records show it's time for your oil change and tire rotation.
- You asked us to notify you when a dance company was performing at the Arts Center.
- As a resident of the Schenk-Atwood Neighborhood, you are directly affected by the recent rise in crime in our area.
- To thank you for your recent purchase at our store, we wanted to invite you to a Sneak Preview Sale.

2. USE THE 11 CREATIVE APPROACHES TO WRITING A FIRST PARAGRAPH FOR PRINT ADS

(Chapter 3, pages 37–42)

- State the most important thing your company, product, or service will do for customers.
- State why they should care about the point you make in the headline and subhead.
- State whom your company serves, what you do, and how you are different.
- Open with a surprising fact.
- Open with a promotional offer.
- Challenge one of the customers' assumptions.
- Open with news.
- State why your topic is timely. Answer the question, "Why now?"

- Show you understand the customers' point of view by describing it.
- Acknowledge a difficult truth and then state why customers need not worry about it.
- Summarize your main persuasive arguments.

3. USE THE FOUR CREATIVE APPROACHES TO WRITING BODY COPY FOR PRINT ADS
(Chapter 3, pages 43–44)

- List multiple features, services, and/or benefits.
- Provide reasons to believe your main claim.
- Give an example.
- Use photos/illustrations and captions.

Letter

In less than half a second your readers (or their secretaries) decide which mail to toss and which to keep. You must get to the point right away with something unexpected or useful. So few people receive letters from friends these days that most letters are automatically assumed to be junk mail.

The outer envelope is the single most important part of the letter, because if the recipients don't open it, nothing inside matters. Envelopes are most likely to be opened if they are handwritten or hand-signed, use a first-class stamp, make a personal reference (computer-personalized), look like a bill or an importance legal notice, or do not look at all like advertising so that they arouse curiosity. Also effective are those envelopes at the opposite end of the spectrum: envelopes that make a clear and compelling promise.

Letters are generally more effective than postcards or brochure mailers. The chief advantage of a letter is that it is personal, from one person to another. Another advantage is that a letter doesn't rely on expensive graphics and you can provide a lot more detail than in a postcard.

There are 15 parts of a marketing letter:

Outer Envelope
1. Front headline
2. Return address
3. Mailing address
4. Indicia
5. Back headline

Letter
6. Address to

7. Address from
8. Headline (optional)
9. Salutation
10. Opening line
11. Body copy
12. Call to action
13. Sign-off
14. Title
15. Postscript

Three things determine the effectiveness of your letter, in order of importance:

1. The quality of your mailing list—Are they names of previous buyers or total strangers? Is the information up to date or outdated?
2. The quality and timing of your offer—Is it new and exciting? Is it different from what's expected? Are customers ready to buy?
3. The quality of the creative execution—Is it clear and well written? Does the design get attention? Is it easy to read?

Your outer envelope is the most critical creative piece, so spend more time thinking about it. Within your letter, the three most important lines are your headline, your opening paragraph line, and your postscript (P. S.).

Time-Saving Tip: You can use almost the same information for your letter as for your print ads, brochures, and postcards: same headline, body copy, call to action, etc. Again, this saves you time and helps build "brand equity."

> While you communicate the same core message in all these mediums, you will want to be more personal in your letter. The best letters are written in the first person, from a person ("I"), working for a company ("we"), to another person ("you").

Dos and Don'ts

- Do make sure you have an excellent mailing list (previous customers, previous interest, updated and current information).
- Do write the letter as personally as possible (use "I," "we," and "you").
- Do have a compelling offer that is both appealing and unexpected.
- Do consider the timing of your mailing. First, check with the Postal Service for an estimate of how long it will take them to deliver your mailing. (This will depend on the size and the range of geographic locations.) Second, mail when customers are ready to buy or beginning to think about what to buy. For example, most Christmas presents are purchased in December. Mailing in February would produce dramatically worse results.
- Do use the same headline and subhead on the front and the back of the envelope. There's a 50/50 chance the recipient will see the back of your envelope first.
- Do look for opportunities to personalize your envelope: handwritten or hand-signed, first-class stamp, or computer-personalized words.
- Do use powerful selling words like *free*, *new*, *now*, *introducing*, and *save*.

- Do avoid general or abstract words like *quality*, *convenience*, *advanced*, *partnership*, and *solutions*.
- Don't reverse out the type in your body copy (white letters on a black background). It can reduce readability by as much as 60%.
- Do make one main point per envelope—and then prove it.
- Do make sure you include a call to action. It can increase results by as much as 20%.
- Don't imitate what your competitors are doing. Do stand out.
- Do check with the Postal Service about sizes, shapes, labels, and postage requirements before you print your envelope.
- Do use split-run testing. (Two versions, different in one major aspect and the contact number. You then measure the difference in results.)

Three Steps to Creating an Envelope

To create your envelope, create the five pieces (page 155) and then put them all together.

Step 1. Create a headline for the front of your envelope.

The headline should state your most important point. It's your hook. If the headline fails, the reader will not open your letter.

Step 2. Add indicia (for mailing in bulk).

Any envelope with a first-class stamp automatically gets more attention. But if you are doing more than several hundred pieces, you will probably need indicia on the upper right of the front of your envelope. The indicia contains postal information (usually a special number or bar code) necessary to send your postcard through the mail at a bulk rate (usually a standard rate or third-class rate). To qualify for this special rate, your pieces must be identical and you generally need to mail at least 500 at a time. You must get your indicia from the Postal Service. The Postal Service is very particular about how the indicia and mailing panel should be laid out on the envelope and what information it should contain. It is also very particular about the size, shape, uniformity, and weight of your mailer.

Get your final envelope layout and information approved by your local Postal Service office before you get your envelope printed. If not and there's a problem, you may need to have your envelopes reprinted.

Step 3. Create a subhead.

You have a choice. You can either duplicate the headline you used on the front or state your second-most important point in a subhead. Use the creative approaches for writing subheads presented in Chapter 2, page 28.

If your headline is really strong, you should put it on the front and on the back of your postcard, because there is a 50/50 chance the recipient will see the back first and read a subhead rather than the strong headline.

If the combination of headline and subhead tells a more complete story that is stronger than the headline alone, then you should put the headline on the front and the subhead on the back.

Four Creative Approaches to Writing an Envelope Headline

1. USE THE 18 CREATIVE APPROACHES TO WRITING A HEADLINE (CHAPTER 2, PAGES 21–27)

2. SUGGEST URGENCY

- Hurry! Offer expires soon.
- Hurry! Offer expires June 21st at 5:00 pm.
- Please open right away. Contains important dated information.
- Contact us before September 23rd or you'll lose your chance to win a 24-foot cabin-cruiser.

3. SUGGEST IMPORTANCE

- Contains important dated information.
- Legal information enclosed (for offers with positive legal impacts).
- Important tax information enclosed (for offers with tax benefits).
- Please review before sending payment.
- Please verify that the enclosed information is correct.
- Personal and confidential.
- Free lottery ticket enclosed (make sure you enclose a ticket).

4. USE NO HEADLINE AT ALL OR IMITATE A NONDE-SCRIPT PERSONAL LETTER TO PROVOKE CURIOSITY

Seven Steps to Creating a Letter

To create your letter, create the six pieces and then put them all together. Most letters are one to two pages long. But length should be determined by the number of new and compelling selling points you can make.

Step 1. Write a headline (optional).

A headline is optional. Your letter can start with a salutation instead. Starting with a headline makes your letter more of an ad and less of a personal letter, but it also gets to the point faster. If you have an important piece of news or a strong benefit or point of difference, you may want to put a headline at the top center of your letter. If you don't use a headline here, you can use it instead at the end of your letter, in the form of a postscript (P.S.).

Step 2. Write the salutation, greeting, or opening sentence of your letter.

- Happy holidays! To make your celebration even merrier, we've added some new gifts.
- Thank you for inquiring about our new CRM-3000 Agitation-Drum Unit.
- Earlier, you indicated you would like to receive information about affordable vacation packages.
- Dear Mr. Smith, to thank you for your patronage, we would like to extend this special service.
- As a valued customer of Denby's, we wanted you to know that our remodeling project will be complete this June.
- Dear Resident, we are opening a new store very close to your house.
- Hello, my name is Barry Callen and I am the founder of Corprov, a Corporate Improv training company.

- On behalf of the Association of Social Services, I'd like to thank you for your past donations.

Step 3. Write body copy.

Every thought should flow naturally from one idea to the other. Your first paragraph should amplify or prove the point you are making in the headline or subhead. Keep it short. Hit the highlights. Then, in the middle of the body, you should provide intriguing or unexpected details. End with a call to action.

Step 4. Create a call to action.

Use the three creative approaches to writing a call to action in Chapter 2, pages 30–31.

- Encourage prospects to act now to avoid losing something.
- Encourage prospects to act now to gain something.
- Encourage prospects to take small, low-risk steps.

Step 5. Sign off your letter.

- Sincerely yours, Bob's Bigger Burger Barn
- Sincerely yours, Barry Callen, Founder, Corprov
- Sincerely yours, Barry Callen, Corprov
- Thank you, Rhonda Pflaum, Customer Service Representative
- We hope to see you soon!
- See you at the party on March 30th! Barry
- Don't hesitate to call if I can be of service.
- If you have any questions, call me at XXX-XXXX.
- Don't miss it! Rollo Viendint, Student Information Coordinator
- Thank you for your consideration. The Staff

Step 6. Add a postscript (P. S.).

Step 7. Assemble all the pieces into a letter.

Check your transitions from sentence to sentence to make sure the logic of your letter flows naturally. If you have a nonsequential list of items to communicate, either number them or use a bullet for each one. Break your text up into the smallest possible paragraphs and use lots of white space. Underline important points. Center or indent quotes, examples, and facts. All of these techniques will make your letter easy to scan. In general, write to a fifth-grade reading level, using simple, short, concrete words.

Four Creative Approaches to Writing Letter Body Copy

1. USE THE 11 CREATIVE APPROACHES TO WRITING A FIRST PARAGRAPH FOR PRINT ADS

(Chapter 3, pages 37–42)

- State the most important thing your company, product, or service will do for customers.
- State why they should care about the point you make in the headline and subhead.
- State whom your company serves, what you do, and how you are different.
- Open with a surprising fact.
- Open with a promotional offer.
- Challenge one of the customers' assumptions.
- Open with news.
- State why your topic is timely. Answer the question, "Why now?"
- Show you understand the customers' point of view by describing it.
- Acknowledge a difficult truth and then state why customers need not worry about it.
- Summarize your main persuasive arguments.

2. USE THE FOUR CREATIVE APPROACHES TO WRITING BODY COPY FOR PRINT ADS

(Chapter 3, pages 43–44)

- List multiple features, services, and/or benefits.
- Provide reasons to believe your main claim.
- Give an example.
- Use photos/illustrations and captions.

3. USE THE EIGHT WAYS TO EMOTIONALLY HOOK LISTENERS IN A RADIO AD

(Chapter 4, pages 97–103)

- Tell a story.
- Quote a person.
- Paint a sensory picture that puts the reader in the scene.
- Dramatize the need.
- List customer choices.
- List features and benefits.
- Describe what is unique or unusual or extreme.
- Contrast the experience you provide with a typical customer experience.

4. USE THE 13 WAYS TO PROVE THAT LISTENERS CAN BELIEVE YOU IN RADIO ADS

(Chapter 4, pages 104–111)

- Prove customer satisfaction.
- Prove leadership.
- Provide a customer testimonial.
- Provide an expert testimonial.
- List credible endorsements.
- List certifications and memberships.
- Offer a guarantee or make-good.
- Prove quality.
- Offer a compelling or unusual statistic, the more precise the better.
- Invite skeptics to see for themselves.
- State a growth fact.
- List years of experience.
- Prove authentic motivation or passion.

Seven Creative Approaches to Writing a Postscript

1. USE THE THREE CREATIVE APPROACHES TO WRITING AN EFFECTIVE CALL TO ACTION
(Chapter 2, pages 30–31)

- Encourage prospects to act now to avoid losing something.
- Encourage prospects to act now to gain something.
- Encourage prospects to take small, low-risk steps.

2. USE THE 17 CREATIVE APPROACHES TO WRITING A PROMOTIONAL OFFER TO ENCOURAGE ACTION
(Chapter 6, pages 228–233)

WARNING: Make sure you check with a lawyer before making any promises or guarantees or claims.

- Create a contest.
- Have a sale.
- Offer freebies.
- Offer savings.
- Feature low prices.
- Provide a free evaluation.
- Offer a rebate or refund.
- Donate to a good cause.
- Make a limited offer, to encourage immediate action.
- Create a savings club.
- Reward specific kinds of customers.
- Turn customers into salespeople.
- Provide free information.
- Reward people for attention.
- Provide a special event.

- Make a guarantee.
- Provide a free sample.

3. REMIND THEM OF AN IMPORTANT REASON TO CARE

- Remember: you have only one week left to take advantage of this offer.
- Until there's a cure, over a million babies a year will die in childbirth worldwide.
- Why put up with an ugly or broken garage door for one more second?
- If you don't volunteer your time for your neighborhood, who else will?
- Remember—the sooner you start your investment program, the sooner you can reach a million dollars net worth.
- If you're not ready to commit to a full purchase at this time, reserve a partial order today, and retain the right for the full discount when and if you make a full purchase.

4. REMOVE ONE OF THEIR OBJECTIONS TO ACTION

- No salesperson will call. We guarantee it.
- You are under no obligation to make a purchase, so feel free to call for information.
- We respect confidentiality. We will not share or sell your name and contact information with anyone else.
- If it doesn't work, return it at no cost to you.
- If you don't like the first edition of our magazine, you can cancel your subscription and keep the complimentary music CD as our way of saying thank you for trying us out.
- If you've been burned before by similar offers, we'll supply you with the name and phone number of a customer in your area who will speak to you candidly.

5. REITERATE A KEY MESSAGE FROM THE BODY OF THE LETTER

Make sure you write it with slightly different words to avoid irritating through repetition.

- Sentence from the body:

    How one old man accidentally invented the fishing lure that revolutionized an industry.

- Reiterate it in the P.S.:

    P.S. Yep, I'm the same fellah who accidentally invented the first bass-biter pheromone lure. (Of course I didn't call it that at the time.)

- Sentence from the body:

    You will get two free lottery tickets with every purchase over $50.

- Reiterate it in the P.S.:

    P.S. Remember, if you order more than $50, we'll give you two free lottery tickets. As I write this letter, the state lottery jackpot is up to $2 million!

- Sentence from the body:

    It's hard to believe, but you could have cancer right now and not even know it!

- Reiterate it in the P.S.:

    P.S. If you do have cancer, the only way to find out is to get tested. Early detection is the key to cancer survival. So get tested now!

6. CROSS-SELL OTHER PRODUCTS OR SERVICES

- Don't forget—we also carry a full line of motorcycle para-phernalia, including leather chaps and stick-on decals.
- The Simul-4500 Laser 3-D Scanner is just one of over 400

laser-based products we sell. Visit our Web site for a full list.

- If you liked My Accountant 9.1, you'll love My Lawyer, My Controller, My Personnel Director, and our 27 other management software products.
- A lot of our customers who buy our terrycloth towels also love our washrags, dishrags, kitchen towels, and bathrobes. Call for a free catalog.
- For only an additional $50, we'll send out an expert to install your new washer and dryer.

7. IF YOU DID NOT USE A HEADLINE IN YOUR LETTER, YOU CAN WRITE A HEADLINE FOR THE P. S.

Use the 18 creative approaches to writing a headline (Chapter 2, pages 21–27).

Sell Sheet / Product Sheet / Specification Sheet

A sell sheet or product sheet or specification sheet is designed to make it easy for your customers to do the following:

1. Compare and choose which products, features, and prices they want,
2. Help sell or reinforce their decision to choose you,
3. Make it easy to represent and explain your product or service to your customers' boss, team members, and purchasing agents,
4. Make it easy to order your product or service,
5. Make it easy to store or file the information for later reference, and
6. Provide a visual aid and leave-behind for your sales staff.

Most sell sheets are printed on one or both sides of an 8½" x 11" single sheet of paper. This makes the sell sheets easy to file, easy to place within the pocket of a standard folder or brochure folder, and easy to add, subtract, or rearrange for a presentation or leave-behind.

Often, the highlights and selling information are put on the front and the more detailed technical specifications and legal information are put on the back. If you include pricing, you may want to put the prices and other highly changeable information on the back and print it in black and white. This will save you money on reprinting costs.

It is not enough to create one sell sheet. You must create a system of sell sheets. The essence of the system is consistency.

There are ten components to an effective sell sheet:

1. Product name and product code
2. Literal category descriptor: what it is and does

3. Photo of product or service
4. Selling headline
5. Highlight paragraph
6. Key features and benefits
7. Table of choices, features and benefits, and prices
8. Contact information
9. Logo and slogan
10. A date, to identify revisions of sell sheets

There are two very different kinds of writing in a sell sheet: *selling words* and *technical words* (specifications/descriptions). Make sure your sell sheet has both. For example:

Selling Words That Create Emotion and Desire

- Nano-Filter captures particulates smaller than .0008 micrometers for the greatest water purity technically possible.

Technical Words That Are Short, Literal, and Descriptive

- Filter type: Nano. Process: Reverse Carbon-Diffusion. Particulate capture: .0008 micrometers. Lifespan: 2,000 gallons. Price: $4,500 US.

Dos and Don'ts

- Do use both selling words and technical words.
- Don't just design one sell sheet. Design a system of sell sheets.
- Do keep your overall design and format and naming systems consistent.
- Do find consistent ways to make each sell sheet predictably different for each different product.
- Do show a photo of your product or service.
- Do create a table that is easily searchable by features, such as price, results, etc.

- Do date your sell sheets so that versions of a sell sheet that are identical except for technical details can be distinguished.
- Do use paper of a size and format that make it easy to file or place in a brochure pocket or folder. Most of the time, this means 8 1/2" x 11".
- Do apply your graphic design standards, if you have them.

11 Steps to Creating a Sell Sheet

To create your sell sheet, create the ten pieces and then put them all together.

Step 1. Write the product name and code.

It is better if you have a system of names and a system of product codes. It is best if the names and product codes have an easy-to-remember logical relationship.

Step 2. Write a literal category descriptor.

This descriptor should tell either what it is and does or what it is and for whom. This is no place for creativity. You want to use the most common, clear, conventional, concrete, literal, and easy-to-understand language possible. This serves as an explanation for your product name.

- Improvisational comedy classes for corporations
- Flower arrangements for weddings
- Six Sigma process redesign for robotic manufacturing
- Commercial roofing, flooring, remodeling, plumbing
- Homemade chocolate chip cookie gift baskets
- Halloween costumes
- Screws, nuts, bolts, and hardware for cabinetry
- Women's health clinic

- Preventing hunger in America
- Biodiesel fuel for truck fleets
- Extreme mountain-biking adventures
- Home water filter for lead, cryptosporidium, particulates, and odors

Step 3. Show photo or illustration of product or service.

- Show a photo of the object
- Show the object in use
- Show a benefit
- Show a type of customer
- Show a demonstration
- Show a technical feature or highlight
- Show an award
- Show a map
- Show the facility or location

Step 4. Write a selling headline.

Use the 18 creative approaches to writing headlines (Chapter 2, pages 21–27).

Step 5. Write a highlights paragraph.

Step 6. List key features and benefits.

Use a subhead or bullet listing format. If you want, you can briefly expand on one or two key points in body copy beneath the features and benefits.

Step 7. Write a table of choices, features and benefits, and prices.

Create a matrix or table, with your products listed down the left and searchable features listed across the top. Think in terms of the categories your customers look for when they shop or make choices. Here are some category possibilities for the top of the matrix.

1. Number of people
- 1 person
- 2 people
- family
- group

2. Dollar amount
- $10–$20
- $20–$30
- $30–$40
- $40–$50
- $50+

3. Special discounts
- Children's discount
- Senior discount
- Group discount

4. Usage
- For camping
- For fishing
- For racing
- For deep-sea diving
- Emergency raft
- Ice-water boating
- For parties

5. Features/services included
- Installation included
- Free one-year safety inspection
- Free 24/7 service line

- Titanium alloy
- Magnetic reinforced locking mechanism
- Fiberdyne ceramic insulator
- Double-sealed safety lining
- Emergency venting system

Step 8. List contact information.

List every conceivable way for your prospect to contact you to ask questions, find out more, or order from you. Highlight one preferred approach by using type size, placement, or boldness. For more information contact:

Barry Callen, Founder, Corpov
Corporate Improv Training
Ph: 608.346.8396
E-mail: barry.callen@gmail.com
Web site: www.barrycallen.com
Fax: XXX.XXX.XXXX
Address: 2720 Sommers Avenue
Madison, Wisconsin 53704

Step 9. Include your logo and slogan.

Generally, your logo should go in the lower right of the page or at the bottom center. Your slogan should generally run either just below your logo or at the bottom of your ad. For a better slogan, use the 23 creative approaches to writing a tagline, a theme line, or a slogan (Chapter 2, pages 13–19).

Step 10. Include a date to identify revisions of sell sheets.

It is better if you have a system of names and a system of product codes. It is best if the two have a logical interrelationship. The best naming systems often use a first and last name: either a different first name with a common last name or vice versa. The best product code systems use meaningful words or phrases within the product name, rather than just using meaningless numbers. This makes the product code easier to remember and adds selling power.

Here are three creative approaches:

- © 6/19/97
- Product Sheet #1114
- Version 7.3

Step 11. Assemble the parts into a sell sheet.

In a sell sheet, you don't have to worry about smooth transitions from section to section. That's because people don't read sell sheets; they scan them, looking for the category of information they want, and only then reading the detail. Make sure you use graphic design to create a clear hierarchy of where the reader's eye should go first, second, third, etc.

In general, put the selling information that will not change much on the front in color, and print the highly changeable technical specs, prices, and dates and updates on the back.

Four Creative Approaches to Writing the Product Name and Code

1. TO CREATE A BETTER BUSINESS OR PRODUCT NAME, USE THE 23 CREATIVE APPROACHES PRESENTED IN CHAPTER 2 (PAGES 13–19).

2. COMBINE A PRODUCT NAME WITH A COMPANY NAME TO CREATE A SERIES OF NAMES AND PRODUCT CODES.

In the examples below, the product names (a class for beginners, a class for selling skills, a class for ideation skills, and a class for power skills) are merged with the company name, Corprov. Using the same "last name" relates the products as a family of products, but using the product name gives each one a unique "first name." Note how the product codes fall naturally out of the product name for easy recall.

NAME	PRODUCT CODE
Beginprov	BP 100
Sellprov	SP 101
Ideaprov	IP 102
Powerprov	PP 103

3. COMBINE A COMPANY NAME AND A PRODUCT NAME TO CREATE A SERIES OF NAMES AND PRODUCT CODES

In the examples below, the company name, Corprov, is merged with the product name (a class for beginners, a class for selling skills, a class for ideation skills, and a class for power skills). Using the same "first name" relates the products as a family of products, but using the product name gives each one a unique "last name." Note how the product codes fall naturally out of the product name for easy recall.

NAME	PRODUCT CODE
Improstart	I-Start 100
Improsell	I-Sell 101
Improstorm	I-Storm 102
Impropower	I-Power 103

4. COMBINE A COMPANY NAME AND A THEME-ORIENTED PRODUCT NAME TO CREATE A SERIES OF NAMES AND PRODUCT CODES

In the examples below, the company name, Corprov, is merged with product names united by a common theme. Using the company name and a common theme unites the products as a single brand family, but using a different theme variant for each product name distinguishes each product. You can use almost any kind of theme to relate your product names. Note how the product codes fall naturally out of the product name for easy recall.

Theme: Target Group

NAME	PRODUCT CODE
Corprov for Beginners	CFB 100
Corprov for Salespeople	CFS 101
Corprov for Creatives	CFC 102
Corprov for Teams	CFT 103

Theme: Purpose

NAME	PRODUCT CODE
Corprov for More Fun	CFMF 100
Corprov for Better Sales	CFBS 101

NAME	PRODUCT CODE
Corprov for More Creativity	CFMC 102
Corprov for Better Morale	CFBM 103

Theme: Animals

NAME	PRODUCT CODE
Corprov for Chickens	Cor-Chick 100
Corprov for Sharks	Cor-Shark 101
Corprov for Peacocks	Cor-Peacock 102
Corprov for Monkeys	Cor-Monkey 103

Theme: Colors

NAME	PRODUCT CODE
Red Corprov	R-prov 100
White Corprov	W-prov 101
Blue Corprov	B-prov 102
Green Corprov	G-prov 103

Two Creative Approaches to Writing a Highlights Paragraph

1. USE THE 11 CREATIVE APPROACHES TO WRITING A FIRST PARAGRAPH FOR PRINT ADS (CHAPTER 3, PAGES 37–42). DO NOT USE THE PROMOTIONAL OFFER

- State the most important thing your company, product, or service will do for customers.
- State why they should care about the point you make in the headline and subhead.
- State whom your company serves, what you do, and how you are different.
- Open with a surprising fact.
- Open with a promotional offer.
- Challenge one of the customers' assumptions.
- Open with news.
- State why your topic is timely. Answer the question, "Why now?"
- Show how you understand the customers' point of view by describing it.
- Acknowledge a difficult truth and then state why customers need not worry about it.
- Summarize your main persuasive arguments.

2. USE THE FOUR CREATIVE APPROACHES TO WRITING BODY COPY FOR PRINT ADS

(Chapter 3, pages 43–44)

- List multiple features, services, and/or benefits.
- Provide reasons to believe your main claim.
- Give an example.
- Use photos/illustrations and captions.

Seven Creative Approaches to Writing Key Features and Benefits

1. BREAK OUT FEATURES AND BENEFITS BY DEPARTMENTS

- Public Relations Department: from event marketing to publicity
- Creative Department: unexpected and relevant ideas for all media
- Media Department: strategic buying for highest ROI
- New Media Department: integrating traditional and Internet media
- Promotions Department: building brands and driving traffic

2. BREAK OUT FEATURES AND BENEFITS BY LIST OF SERVICES

- Architectural Design to build your dream home
- Carpentry with sturdy materials and precision finish
- Painting that is neat, clean, and professional
- Roofing that will last the life of your house
- Plumbing that won't cost an arm and a leg
- Electrical to bring your house up to safety codes

3. BREAK OUT FEATURES AND BENEFITS BY PRODUCTS

- Centralized data repository for system-wide real-time updating
- Accounting software to improve billing and cash flow
- Work flow/scheduling software to reduce turnaround
- Alert software to prevent problems
- Modeling software to standardize best-practices system-wide

4. BREAK OUT FEATURES AND BENEFITS BY PRODUCT LINES

- Lawn and garden tools that decrease physical effort
- Craft tools and supplies that are intuitive to use
- Small equipment rental for amateur use
- Heavy equipment for heavy-duty professional use

5. BREAK OUT FEATURES AND BENEFITS BY TARGET MARKETS

- Infant formula helps babies thrive
- Children's supplements taste good so they take them more easily
- Athletic performance enhancers without steroids
- Diabetic nutritional products that taste like normal food
- Sterile intravenous solutions for immune-compromised adults

6. BREAK OUT FEATURES AND BENEFITS BY PROBLEM AREAS

- Cardiac Center has performed the most surgeries in the area
- Cancer Center rated among the nation's best
- Neo-natal Intensive Care Unit uses state-of-the-art technology
- 20 Primary Care Centers for convenient access
- Mental Health Residential Program for addiction and trauma

7. BREAK OUT FEATURES AND BENEFITS BY PRICE OR SIZE

- For towns with fewer than 1,000 people
- For towns with 1,000–10,000 people
- For towns with 10,000–50,000 people
- For towns with 50,000–100,000 people
- For towns with more than 100,000 people
- One-day weekday escapes for under $140 per person
- Friday/Saturday Funday Family Cruise: $200 for five people
- Three-day weekend getaways for $300 per person
- Seven-day safaris for two only $1,000 total

Chapter 6
Tactics for Catalog Copy, Invitations, Coupons, and Promotions

Catalog Product Description

Customers read catalogs in order to choose the products they wish to order. A catalog is the printed equivalent of a retail store, with products organized into sections, aisles, and shelves. You will want to create some sort of design that enables your readers to quickly find the sections of interest to them. You can organize your sections by product group, type of customer, situation or need, price, or order number. You can also color code the sections on the top or side of the page to make it easier for customers to find what they want.

Like real estate for retail stores, catalog space is precious. You want to give more space and premier space to your best-selling products. You want to highlight specials and deals. Often this is done with "bursts"—small explosions, stars, or circles that contain special or exciting promotional information. Be careful you don't use too many promotional bursts or they will cease to be special and just become clutter. There are eight aspects to catalog product descriptions:

1. Benefit Headline	Improve team morale and creativity
2. Photo of Product	GROUP OF EMPLOYEES LAUGHING AND JUMPING
3. Photo Caption (Optional)	Play is the most effective way to learn.
4. Product Description	Motivate your team and restore morale by playing improv games together. You'll have so much fun you won't even realize you are learning better collaboration, listening, creativity, and presentation skills. No special skills are required, so everyone can play. Four hours flies by when you're laughing and learning.
5. Promotional Offer (Optional)	Hurry! Class size limited.
6. Item Number/ Order Number	Improv 101A
7. Price	$2500 for a half day. Maximum: 40 people.
8. Bottom-of-Page Ordering Information	Call 608 347-8396 now!

Catalog Cover

The cover of your catalog is critical. It tells the customers what "store" they are entering. As with a retail store window, you want to showcase your best merchandise in the best way to entice the readers into the catalog. And you want a big clear sign on the front of the store (the front cover) that shows your store name (your logo) and identifies what you do (a category descriptor under your name).

On the inside cover or in the first few pages, you might want to sell the store itself (your company), rather than the products. You can use a summary of what makes your company or products different. You can show customer endorsements and testimonials. You can even include a letter from the president of your company.

If your catalog exceeds four pages, you might also consider an index or table of contents, so the customer can go right to the products that interest them. This is the equivalent of a store directory or a customer service person at the front door.

You will also want a section in the center or at the back of your catalog that contains ordering and service information. It might include order forms, phone numbers, and Web site URLs. You will also want to make it easy for the customers to order directly from the page on which a product item appears. So it is a good idea to put the phone number or URL at the bottom of every two-page spread. That way, the second that customers see a product they like, they can order it immediately. This increases response.

But the heart and soul of your catalog are your product descriptions. These generally should not exceed one paragraph. Keep them short, descriptive, and exciting. Don't state the obvious or try to do the job of the photo. Make sure your headline addresses a need or touts a benefit. Let the product photo describe as much of the detail as possible, so that you can save your writing for the important points that are not so obvious. If there's room, a photo caption is worth its weight in gold, because it is highly read. Treat it just like a subhead. It should not repeat the headline, but it should make your second-most important point.

The goal of your catalog product description is not to build awareness or interest. It is to generate an order right now.

Dos and Don'ts

■ Do limit each product description to one short paragraph, if possible.

■ Do give more space and better catalog locations to your best-selling products or services.

■ Do keep your overall design and format and organization consistent.

■ Do place phone numbers and Web site URLs on every page, to make it easy to order.

■ Do show a photo of your product or service.

■ Do use a photo caption to communicate your second-most important benefit.

■ Do create a table that is easily searchable by features such as price, purpose, etc.

■ Don't keep running product descriptions that don't sell. Change the mailing list, the product, the offer (price/benefit/promotion), or the descriptions. Use split-run copy testing to find out which ads are pulling harder.

■ Don't use empty adjectives, such as *exciting*, *amazing*, *vibrant*. Instead, use active verbs, such as *rings*, *zaps*, *relaxes*, *eliminates*.

■ Do ask yourself, "What would I want to know about this product in order to buy it?" Then write about that.

■ Do ask yourself, "What makes this product unique or different?" Write about that.

- Don't state the obvious. Everyone knows a cup has a handle, especially if a photo shows one.
- Do create a standardized visual system for communicating information common to most products. For example, make sure different ads use the same type and placement and graphic device for item number, price, or color.

Creative Tip: Select words to convey your company's or product's personality, voice, or feeling. That way you go beyond supplying information and you engage the readers' emotions. This will make them care more and want to buy.

Here is the same product with the same basic details, described in three ways that evoke very different feelings.

SOLID, DEPENDABLE NO-NONSENSE PERSONALITY:

- 4-hour class. 10 different improv games. No special equipment or skills required. Up to 40 students per class.

SMART BUSINESS STYLE:

- Motivate your team and restore morale by playing improv games together. Your employees will have so much fun they won't even realize they are learning better collaboration, listening, creativity, and presentation skills. No special acting or comedy talents are required, so everyone can play. Four hours fly by when you're laughing and learning.

CREATIVE, FUN PERSONALITY:

- Holy cow! Is that silent Bob from accounting pretending to be a talking pretzel?
- Anyone who can walk and talk can do improv games. And they won't even realize they are improving their abilities to collaborate, listen, create, and present to a group. Laughing and learning sure beats four hours of PowerPoint slides!

Six Steps to Creating a Catalog Product Description

To create your catalog product description, create the four pieces of your description and then put them all together. Then, in step 6, write the information on how to order. Order information should be placed at the bottom of each catalog page for all the products to share.

Step 1. Write a benefit-oriented headline.

- Super-flexible dust control for woodshops
- Improve team morale and creativity
- Drop a Mountain of Candy Memories on Grandma and Grandpa

Step 2. Write a product description.

Step 3. Use photo captions to highlight secondary benefit (optional).

You don't have to have a photo or a caption, but they will attract above-average attention and interest, particularly if there is a powerful visual demonstration or a feature you want to highlight. You can use your caption just like a subhead, to communicate your second-most important point.

Step 4. Highlight special promotional offers (optional).

You can highlight special promotional offers. Make sure you don't do this on every product or your offers will cease to be special.

Step 5. Combine the elements into a single paragraph.

HEADLINE:	Super-flexible dust control for woodshops
PHOTO:	HOSE STUCK TO A WALL
CAPTION:	Suction so powerful it can stick to a bare wall!

DESCRIPTION: 20 hose branching pickup points, one-click male/female gates, 7.5 hp dust collector, four-room maximum capacity.

PROMOTIONAL
HIGHLIGHT: Product # 53: New!

HEADLINE: Improve team morale and creativity
PHOTO: GROUP OF EMPLOYEES LAUGHING AND JUMPING
CAPTION: Play is the most effective way to learn.
DESCRIPTION: Motivate your team and restore morale by playing improv games together. You'll have so much fun you won't even realize you're learning better collaboration, listening, creativity, and presentation skills. No special skills are required, so everyone can play. Four hours flies by when you're laughing and learning.

PROMOTIONAL
HIGHLIGHT: Hurry! Class size limited.

HEADLINE: Drop a Mountain of Candy Memories on Grandma and Grandpa
PHOTO: A HUGE DROP-SHAPED TIN FILLED WITH CANDY
CAPTION: "Omigosh! Look what the kids sent us, honey!"
DESCRIPTION: Show them how much you love them with a whopping five lbs. of five classic candy drops. Give them back memories of savory cinnamon Christmases, tart sunny lemon summertimes, juicy windowsill cherry pies, luscious whole-some milk chocolate and exotic bittersweet dark chocolate. Drop-shaped checkerboard gift tin is a special keepsake all by itself.

PROMOTIONAL
HIGHLIGHT: Item No. 395683A Was $51.36. NOW $46.17

Step 6. Write ordering information for the bottom of the page.

- Call toll-free 24/7. Operators are standing by to help. 1-800-XXX-XXXX.
- Call 608 347 8396 now. Or order online: barry.callen@gmail.com
- Mail in your order today. Postage-paid order forms on page 11.

Three Creative Approaches to Highlighting Special Promotional Offers

1. USE COLOR AND/OR BOLD, UNDERLINED, OR ITALICIZED TYPE TO HIGHLIGHT INFORMATION

- Item No. 395683A Was $51.36. **NOW $46.17**
- Product # 53: <u>New!</u>
- Aquamarine Percale Sheets: *Hurry! Supplies limited.*

2. PLACE PROMOTIONAL LANGUAGE INSIDE AN ICON OR SPECIAL BORDER

INSIDE STARBURST: 50% OFF!

INSIDE CARTOON BALLOON: Free with purchase!

SCISSORS/PRICETAG ICON: Price-Cutter Special!

3. USE THE 17 CREATIVE APPROACHES TO PROMOTION (PRESENTED LATER IN THIS CHAPTER) TO ENCOURAGE ACTION

WARNING: Make sure you check with a lawyer before making any promises, guarantees, or claims.

- Create a contest.
- Have a sale.
- Offer freebies.
- Offer savings.
- Feature low prices.
- Provide a free evaluation.
- Offer a rebate or refund.
- Donate to a good cause.
- Make a limited offer, to encourage immediate action.
- Create a savings club.
- Reward specific kinds of customers.

- Turn customers into salespeople.
- Provide free information.
- Reward people for attention.
- Provide a special event.
- Make a guarantee.
- Provide a free sample.

Three Examples of Catalog Elements Put into a Single Paragraph

EXAMPLE 1

HEADLINE: **Super-flexible dust control for woodshops**

PHOTO: HOSE STUCK TO A WALL

CAPTION: Suction so powerful it can stick to a bare wall!

DESCRIPTION: 20 hose branching pickup points, one-click male/female gates, 7.5 hp dust collector, four-room maximum capacity.

PROMOTIONAL
HIGHLIGHT: Product # 53: *New!*

EXAMPLE 2

HEADLINE: **Improve team morale and creativity**

PHOTO: GROUP OF EMPLOYEES LAUGHING AND JUMPING

CAPTION: Play is the most effective way to learn.

DESCRIPTION: Motivate your team and restore morale by playing improv games together. You'll have so much fun you won't even realize you're learning better collaboration, listening, creativity, and presentation skills. No special skills are required, so everyone can play. Four hours flies by when you're laughing and learning.

PROMOTIONAL
HIGHLIGHT: *Hurry! Class size limited.*

EXAMPLE 3

HEADLINE: **Drop a Mountain of Candy Memories on Grandma and Grandpa**

PHOTO: A HUGE DROP-SHAPED TIN FILLED WITH CANDY

CAPTION: "Omigosh! Look what the kids sent us, honey!"

DESCRIPTION: Show them how much you love them with a whopping five lbs. of five classic candy drops. Give them back memories of savory cinnamon Christmases, tart sunny lemon summertimes, juicy windowsill cherry pies, luscious wholesome milk chocolate and exotic bittersweet dark chocolate. Drop-shaped checker board gift tin is a special keepsake all by itself.

PROMOTIONAL
HIGHLIGHT: Item No. 395683A Was $51.36. **NOW $46.17**

Invitations

Invitations can be either general or individual. The more individ-ualized and the more personalized, the greater the response. A handwritten invitation with an individual's name on it will pull more response than a postcard addressed to a business organi-zation, especially if it is a signed personal invitation from an indi-vidual the recipient knows. But if your target market is in the thousands, such as a trade show invitation, handwritten invita-tions may be impractical.

There are five elements to an invitation:

1. Request for Attendance	You are cordially invited to
2. Event	the Annual Improv Training Showcase
3. Featuring	featuring the improv com-edy of Without Annette.
4. Date/Time/Place	Feb. 25, 2010 Blascau Theatre
5. Call to Action	Limited free seating. Please RSVP by Feb. 23 to 608 555-1456

The event itself is more critical to success than the invitation. The more unique, useful, exclusive, expensive, or entertaining the event, the greater the response will be. Make sure you lead with the most compelling detail. For example, if a celebrity is signing autographs, make that the centerpiece of the event. Free food and drink also increase the number attending. The timing and location of the event are also critical. Is it being held at an exclusive country club or in an office building? Is it sched-uled at the same time as a popular keynote speaker's address? Is it a short easy walk from the main floor of the trade show or does it require an expensive 30-minute taxi ride?

What you name the event can make a big difference in attendance. If the event is intended to be educational, call it a seminar. If it is intended to be fun, call it a party. Or perhaps it's an open bar, a beach trip, a roundtable discussion, a colloquium, or a clients-only celebration. You must quickly answer the question, "What kind of event is it?" Don't be afraid to be creative and memorable in naming your event.

Make sure you have an up-to-date mailing list of the kind of people who would be interested in your event.

There is usually an optimal window of time for the invitation to appear. Too soon and invited guests might forget it. Too late and they are already booked. Allow time for the mailing to reach the target. You may even want to send an earlier mailing asking them to "hold the date." Multiple mailings will draw more people. A good rule of thumb is to send an invitation three times. Just make sure you don't send it again to people who have already signed on. Some mailers like to put a small hedge line in the body copy: "Our apologies if you have already RSVP'd."

Invitation formats vary considerably. Invitations can be in the form of a postcard, a standard business letter, or an expensive wedding-style envelope and card. You can either require an RSVP in order to better plan your event or leave the invitation open in order to allow people to show up at the last minute.

You can go into great detail about what is exciting about the event. You can even include photos of performers or last year's party crowd.

Whatever your format, the heart of an invitation is essentially a single poster-type headline that contains a request for attendance; the event name and description; a compelling feature of the event; the date, time, and place of the event; and (optional) a call to action. If this key line does not catch your potential guest's attention, the rest of the details won't matter. So put the invitation line front and center. And put the details in the back.

Creative Tip: Unless you have a huge mailing, it is a good idea to make your invitation as personal and unique as possible. Here are some ways to do that:

- Handwrite the invitation.
- Use the individual's name and title.
- Sign your name and title.
- Computer-personalize the letter with names and details.
- Handwrite a note on the printed invitation (but do it only if the invitation is inside an envelope or you may not qualify for a bulk mailing rate from the Postal Service).
- Use "wedding-style" stationery: heavier stock, unusual colors and textures, gold embossing, deckled (artfully torn) edges, transparent vellum overleaf, gold braiding, special binding, non-standard envelope shape. (Check with the Postal Service first to make sure it doesn't affect your mailing costs.)
- Use a gothic or script-style typeface.
- Enclose a free gift item, such as a drink ticket or a raffle ticket.
- Use a three-dimensional mailer (a box) containing unusual objects, such as noisemakers, party hats, snacks, etc. Usually this is done for your premier prospects only, such as your top 100 customers. You can send a mass mailing to the others in your target group.
- Have the invitation telegraphed, text-messaged, Fedexed, sent special delivery, or hand-delivered.

Dos and Don'ts

- Do make sure you have an excellent mailing list (previous customers, previous interest, updated and current information).
- Do make sure your event is compelling, unusual, exclusive, useful, or entertaining.
- Do offer food and drink, if possible.
- Do check to make sure the location and hour of your event are convenient and that the date is clear of competing events.
- Do give your event an unexpected, relevant, and ownable name that you can use year after year.
- Do personalize your invitation as much as possible.
- Do highlight a key or compelling or unique feature of the event in the main headline.
- Don't send your invitations out too early or too late.
- Do send out invitations more than once, preferably three times.
- Don't resend an invitation to someone who has already signed up.
- Don't clutter up the main invitation headline with details. Put the headline front and center on its own page. Put the details inside the invitation or on the back.
- Do consider unusual mailing formats such as three-dimensional boxes and unusual methods of delivery such as text-messaging or telegrams.

Six Steps to Creating an Invitation

To develop your invitation, create the five elements of your main headline and then put them all together.

Invitations Step 1. Request Attendance

- You are cordially invited to attend ...
- Please RSVP for ...
- Don't miss ...
- Announcing ...
- Stop by ...
- Reserve a seat for ...
- Get your tickets now for ...
- Only a select few are invited to ...
- You and one guest are invited to attend ...
- Corprov Corporate Improv invites you to ...
- Attention, antique automobile lovers! You're invited to ...
- Save the date for ...
- Call now to RSVP for ...
- Enclosed is your private access code to participate in ...
- It's time once again for ...
- You've never seen anything like ...

Invitations Step 2. Name/Describe the Event

The name of your event can make a big difference in attendance. For example, the name "Envirothon 2010" might be more ownable and memorable than the more generic "Walkathon to Protect the Environment." For a better name, see the creative tips presented in Chapter 2, pages 7–11. Here are some examples:

- a City Symphony performance of The Nutcracker
- an improv comedy show starring Without Annette
- pre-show cocktails
- dinner and dancing at the Savoy
- free wine and hors d'oeuvres
- one-hour meet-and-greet
- "welcome new customers" party
- Diamond Club members banquet
- members-only gathering
- speech by noted author Barry Callen
- seminar on "How to Make a Million in Real Estate"
- roundtable discussion of "Third-World Poverty—Towards a Solution"
- Webinar on "Measuring Outgassing in Plastic Compression Modules"
- our annual awards banquet
- celebrity roast of our departing mayor
- sneak preview of our new product line
- trunk show of the latest titanium eyeglasses from Paris
- grand opening of our latest retail outlet
- celebrate our first ten million in sales

- beach volleyball party
- silent auction for charity
- Rewards Customers Midnight Sale
- our annual family picnic
- a Walkathon to Protect the Environment
- volunteer thank-you party
- the Annual Company Blood Drive for Employees
- our weekly Lunch-and-Learn

Invitations Step 3. Highlight a Key Feature (Optional)

- starring world-renowned Romanian violinist "Vladimir Ptoskenanimov"
- (voted Best Comedy Group in the City for three years in a row)
- open bar
- at the exclusive Kettle Club Backroom
- best-selling author of Perfect Phrases for Marketing Communications
- trade-only
- moderated by world-recognized expert, Professor Nancy Stair
- (see the new silicon chip you've been hearing about)
- (including a runway show, a short talk by the designer, and a raffle)
- (toys, prizes, music, games, balloons, and amazing discounts)
- (and take home a free bottle of Dom Pérignon)
- (we've trucked in two tons of beach sand)
- to help the victims of Hurricane Katrina
- (exclusive deals exclusively for our rewards customers)
- (we'll supply everything but your family)
- (save a life and we'll save some food and drinks for you)
- This week's topic: "How to use those darned shortcut keys"

Invitations Step 4. Briefly List the Date, Time, and Place of the Event

- 222 Main Street, Baxter Building, 23rd floor
  4/25/09 5:00–10:00 PM.
- When: 10 AM–6 PM, Saturday Only, 4/13/11
  Where: Corner of Main and Smithson, near the West
  Centre Mall
- Time: 6:30 PM–8:00 PM
  Date: Sat. June 16, 2007
  Place: Lulu's Glasses Emporium
  2302 Willard Avenue
  Stoughton, Maryland
  Call 1-800-XXX-XXXX for directions

Invitations Step 5. Call the Potential Guests to Action (Optional)

- RSVP Required.
- Please RSVP to Barry Callen at 608 347 8396 before June 13th.
- Reserve tickets online now. First come, first served. www.barry.callen@gmail.com.
- Seating is limited, so sign up now. Call tollfree 1-800-XXX-XXXX.
- Regrets only.
- Don't miss your chance to see this rare event.
- Hurry! Reservations must be made before 5:00 p.m. 12/22/09.
- To get in, tell 'em Barry sent you.
- Bring a blanket and a picnic lunch.
- Sign-up sheet in the main lobby by the seating area.
- Call today and we'll mail you your ticket.
- $50 in advance. $75 at the door.

Invitations Step 6. Combine the Five Steps into an Invitation on a Single Page

Use graphics and typography to highlight the name of the event and, if appropriate, one key selling feature. Most invitations are center-justified and placed on a single facing page.

Don't miss
The Grand Opening
of our latest Duct Tape World outlet
Where: Corner of Main and Smithson,
near the West Centre Mall
When: 10 AM–6 PM, Saturday Only, 4/13/11
Toys, prizes, music, games, balloons, and amazing discounts!

You and one guest are cordially invited to attend
A Trunk Show of the Latest Titanium Eyeglasses from Paris
(including a runway show, a short talk
by the designer, and a raffle)
Time: 6:30 PM–8:00 PM
Date: Sat. June 16, 2007
Place: Lulu's Spectacle Emporium
2302 Willard Avenue
Stoughton, Maryland
Call 1-800-XXX-XXXX for directions
RSVP Required

Enclosed is your private access code to participate in
**The Acme Corporation Webinar on
"Measuring Outgassing in
Plastic Compression Modules,"
moderated by world-recognized expert,
Professor Nancy Stair**
Register online at
www.outgasplasticcompression.com/webinar by 9.20.07.
Thursday only. 9.23.07, 1:00–3:00 PM EST
Limit one participant per access code. By invitation only.

You are cordially invited to
**The Annual Improv Training Showcase
featuring the improv comedy of *Without Annette*.**
Feb. 25, 2010
Blascau Theatre
Limited free seating. Please RSVP by Feb. 23.
608.347.8396

Coupons

The primary purpose of a coupon is to encourage people to try something immediately. For customers who are on the bubble, a coupon offer can push them to act now. For regular customers, a coupon can be used to cross-sell them to new products, to upsell them to more expensive products, or to get them to purchase more frequently.

The great danger of coupons is that they can become addictive. You offer coupons and sales go up in the short term. But over time, the result can be to accustom customers to expect coupons and discounts. As a result, they wait to purchase until you offer a coupon or they become resentful if you don't offer a discount. This cheapens the perception of your brand's value.

There are six parts of a coupon:

1. Promotional Offer	This coupon is good for One Hour of Free Instruction in Improvisational Comedy
2. Product Name/Company	by Corprov: Corporate Improv Training Name/Logo
3. Photo/Illustration (Optional)	PHOTO: INSTRUCTOR AND STUDENTS JUMPING AROUND LAUGHING
4. Description/Selling Line (Optional)	Anyone can do it, including you! Improve your collaboration, creativity, listening, and presentation skills.
5. Redemption Directions/ Location	Coupon Code #: Imprv66apple2. E-mail your coupon code number and your

contact information to Barry Callen at barry.callen@ gmail.com and I'll notify you of the next available one-hour demonstration class in your area.

6. Limitations/Legal Disclaimers/ Expiration Date

Class size is limited and on a first-come, first-served basis, so reserve your spot today. Offer expires 10/10/09.

WARNING: Coupons and promotional offers make promises you must be prepared to legally defend. Laws vary by jurisdiction and industry. Consult with your lawyer before printing and distributing any coupon.

Coupons ultimately favor the largest and best-funded competitors, because they have the financial resources and the volume to be able to lower their profits for a longer time.

Make sure your coupon matches your brand. For products or services that cost over $100, it's generally better to discount by a percentage. For products or services under $100, it's generally better to discount by a cash amount. If you have a prestige or luxury brand, think twice about doing any kind of coupon.

Customers vary in their use of coupons. There are "professional coupon collectors" who chase the biggest coupon savings and will not become long-term loyal customers. There are people who dislike coupons and refuse to use them at all. And there are folks in between, who use coupons occasionally, especially for specific kinds of products and services.

The best coupons are pleasant surprises that offer something unusual. Customers perceive them as rare gifts rather than taking them for granted.

Dos and Don'ts

- Don't distribute coupons without first checking with your lawyer to get the wording and disclaimers approved.
- Do look at your competitors' coupons and use their legal limitation copy as a starting point for your "fine print."
- Do look at your competitors' coupons and find a way to exceed or differentiate from their offers.
- Coupons can create sudden spikes in traffic, usually within the first few hours and days after they are distributed. Make sure your store personnel and phone lines are ready to handle any increase in volume.
- Don't offer coupons on low-quality or bad products or services. The more people try your products or services and have a bad experience, the more likely they are to avoid you permanently.
- Don't send the same coupons to your current customers as you send to entice new customers. You could lose money by selling for less to current customers who are willing to pay full price. Instead, try to sell current customers up to a higher dollar amount or greater frequency of purchase.
- Do use coupons and discounts to encourage new customers to try your products or services.
- Don't offer coupons constantly or you will train your customers to wait on purchasing until you provide a coupon or, worse, to always expect a special deal.

- Do try to design an offer that not only offers a deal, but builds your brand perception of quality. For example, a free product trial can build brand perception but 10% off the price can cheapen it.
- Don't offer a discount on a luxury or prestige product. It will cheapen the perception of your brand. Instead, offer an additional object or experience that enhances the perception of luxury and prestige.
- Do use coupons to test promotional offers. Use split-run printings (where every other coupon has a different offer) to see which offer pulls the most responses.

Six Steps to Creating a Coupon

To create your coupon, create the five pieces of your coupon copy and then put them all together.

Coupons Step 1. Write a Promotional Headline

Make sure you highlight the financial offer with typography or color. You can also use a dollar-bill graphic design format to repeat the numbers of your offer. Here's an example. This is your headline:

Present this coupon and
Save up to 50%
at our Grand Opening Sale

You could also put a "Save 50%" line in one oval border on the left and one oval border on the right of the coupon. So your customers would see the following.

SAVE		SAVE
50%		50%

Present this coupon and
SAVE UP TO 50%
at Our Grand Opening Sale

Seven Creative Approaches to Writing a Promotional Headline for a Coupon

1. CREATE A COUPON FOR A SALE

This coupon is good for
**One Hour of Free Instruction
in Improvisational Training
Games for Corporations**

Present this coupon and
save up to 50%
at our Grand Opening Sale.

St. Patrick's Day Clothing Sale.
50% off anything green
with this coupon.

Use this coupon to
Buy one, Save 10%
at our 1/10 Sale.

Present this coupon and
Save up to 40%
at our Annual Clearance Sale.

To thank you for your business,
here's a coupon good for
$10 off any purchase
during our Thank-You Sale.

2. OFFER FREEBIES

This coupon good for
one free helium balloon
per child.

Free calculator!

To say thanks for your business,
we'd like to give you
10% off your next purchase.

Yes, I would like to get a
free annual subscription
to ___ Magazine—
worth over $25.
Name: _____
Address: _____
Phone: _____

Get a free air freshener
with your purchase of
a premium car wash.

Free ice cream
when you order a Child's Mealbox.

Present this coupon when you
upgrade your ticket and enjoy
full VIP Club privileges
for one day.

3. OFFER SAVINGS

Get 10% off
your next purchase.

$1.00 off
your next purchase.

Save $10
on every $100 of material you buy.

To thank you for your business,
we'd like to give you a
20% discount
on your next purchase.

Buy 10. Save 10%
With this coupon.

Why pay full price when you can
save $40?

15% off the list price.

Enjoy a 20% discount
on any order over $200
with this coupon.

4. OFFER A FREE EVALUATION

Fill out this coupon
and we'll give you a
free painting estimate.

Mail in your answers to this brief questionnaire
and we'll give you
**three insurance options
and a recommendation at no charge.**

5. OFFER A REBATE OR REFUND

You can offer cash or rebates and get creative by formatting
the coupon to look like a check.

Buy now and we'll send you
a check for $100.

Present this coupon for a
$400 rebate
on purchases of $1000 or more.

Get a 46% rebate
with this coupon.

To thank you for your business,
here is a $10 refund check.

Get a $20 manufacturer's rebate.

6. PROVIDE FREE INFORMATION

Send in this coupon for a
free 10-page brochure,
"How to Grow Bigger Tomatoes."

Mail in this coupon for a
free home self-test kit.

Type in this access code to download
"100 Tips for More Effective Sales Presentations"
free
at www. freetips.com.

7. OFFER A FREE SAMPLE

Present this coupon for a
free sample of our new perfume.

Complete this online form for a
free sample of our new MaxMax sandpaper,
courtesy of Maxon Industries.

Use this online coupon to
download one free song from our band
at www.ourband.com.

Good for
one free sample at Owens Delicatessen
this Thursday only.

Coupons Step 2. Write Description or Selling Line (Optional)

Briefly indicate what is wonderful about your offer in order to entice your customer to act.

SHOWING YOUR OFFER IS WONDERFUL

- Anyone can do it. Improve your collaboration, creativity, listening, and presentation skills.
- Toys, Prizes, Games, Balloons, Food, Refreshments, Clowns, and Family Entertainment.
- Enjoy the biggest juiciest tomatoes of all, regardless of your soil conditions.
- Find out if there is lead in your bloodstream—before it's too late.
- Equivalent to a $500 seminar!
- Muramonix 5000 handheld calculates interest rates and income. A $40 value!
- The Main Magazine for the Extreme Skier.
- Your choice of scents: pine, vanilla, musk, citrus, or jasmine.
- Good for two scoops of our flavor of the day, plus two toppings.
- VIP treatment includes concierge, comfort lounge, complimentary drinks, fax, and Internet connection.
- That's DOUBLE the average discount!
- You may have too little insurance—or too much! Find out for free.
- We like to treat our customers well.
- An original fragrance for the adventurous woman from The House of [French designer].

Coupons Step 3. Show Where or How the Customers Can Redeem the Coupon

Do this if you haven't done it in the headline.

- Offer good at all Spumonti's Southern Shoe Barns. Call 1-800-XXX-XXXX for locations and hours.

- Redeemable at any participating perfume purveyor. Visit our Web site at www.chainofscents.com for the store nearest you.

- Barry Callen is located at 720 Sommers Avenue, Madison, WI 53704.

- Corner of Wilson and Evergreen, just south of the Barrymore Theater.

- E-mail your coupon code number and your contact information to Barry Callen at barry.callen@gmail.com and I'll notify you of the next available demonstration class in your area.

- To participate in our Webinar, visit our Web site anytime before 5 PM 9/23/08 at www.outgasplasticcompression. com/webinar and type in this access code: GE45Tm72.

Coupons Step 4. Limit Your Offer to Encourage Immediate Action

In this way, you avoid assuming an obligation for life and you limit your legal exposure. Check with your lawyer before printing.

- Offer expires 9/25/09.
- Hurry! Supplies are limited. Offer void after 10/17/08.
- Sign up today. Class size is limited. Offer expires 12/30/08.
- Only the first 100 customers to sign up for gym membership will get a free massage.
- Hurry! Offer ends at 5 pm this Saturday, 4/14/07.
- Don't miss the last day of our annual coupon sale or you'll have to wait another 361 days.
- At these prices, these motorcycles won't last long. So come in today. Or at least before the offer expires on 5/06/11.
- Don't wait and miss out. Call now and reserve your seat at a discount with your credit card.

Coupons Step 5. Make Sure to Include Legal Disclaimers

Generally, these disclaimers are placed in small type in a spot where they are least likely to be read. However, some states and industries have restrictions on how small the type can be or where disclaimers must be placed. Because regulations vary by jurisdiction and product category, *make sure to check with your lawyer first* before printing your legal disclaimers.

- Offer expires 11/04/12 at midnight.
- Void where prohibited by law.
- Offer good only with purchase of $100 or more at a participating store.
- Offer prohibited in the following states: Ohio and Alaska.
- Available only at participating dealers.
- Limit one per customer.
- May not be used in conjunction with any other coupon or discount.
- ID required for proof of eligibility.
- Supplies are limited and will be made available on a first-come, first-served basis.
- See your local dealer for details.
- Some limitations may apply.
- Visit our Web site at www.ourwebsite.com for details.
- $25 minimum purchase required.
- Limit one per family.
- Physical activity is required. If you have a health issue, check with your doctor before participating.
- Consult your physician before using this product.

- You must be 18 years or older to order this product. Proof of age required.
- Questions? Call us at 1-800-XXX-XXXX.

Coupons Step 6. Assemble the Parts into a Single Coupon

This coupon is good for
**One Hour of Free Instruction
in Improvisational Training
Games for Corporations**

Anyone can do it, including you! Improve your collaboration, creativity, listening, and presentation skills.
PHOTO: INSTRUCTOR AND STUDENTS JUMPING AROUND LAUGHING
Coupon Code #: Imprv66apple2
E-mail your coupon code number and your contact information to Barry Callen at barry.callen@gmail.com and I'll notify you of the next available one-hour demonstration class in your area. Class size is limited and on a first-come, first-served basis, so reserve your spot today. Offer expires 10/10/09.

Present this coupon and
**save up to 50%
at our Grand Opening Sale**
This Saturday and Sunday only: 10 AM to 5 PM.
LOGO: STORE NAME
INSET VISUAL: MAP SHOWING STORE LOCATION
Toys, Prizes, Games, Balloons, Food, Refreshments, Clowns, and Family Entertainment.
103 Caucona Drive, Corner of Smith and Main, near the Southtown Mall.
Limit: one coupon per customer. May not be combined with other coupons or sale prices. Offer expires 01/23/08.

Free calculator!

When you open a checking account with a $1000 minimum.
PHOTO OF CALCULATOR.

Muramonix 5000 handheld calculates interest rates and income. A $40 value!

Stop by any BankerBank branch before 04/05/09.

FDIC-insured. Equal Opportunity Lender. $1000 minimum balance required. Some penalties may apply. Calculator available while supplies last. Limit: one calculator per new account and per customer. BankerBank employees are ineligible. Some limitations may apply. See your local BankerBank branch director for details.

Yes, I would like to get a
**free one-year subscription
to SLOPEDOPE Magazine—
worth over $25.**

Name: _____

Address: _____

Phone: _____

E-mail: _____

The Main Magazine for the Extreme Skier

Mail this coupon to SLOPEDOPE Magazine, 1 Ski Breeze Pike, Suite 1010, Mountain, Colorado, 80910. Offer good in the continental United States only. You must be 18 years of age. Offer expires 10/09/08.

Present this coupon for a
$400 rebate
on purchases of $1000 or more
for any industrial metal-polishing applications.
It's our way of saying thank you.

Call your sales representative at 1-800-XXX-XXXX and place your order. Offer expires XX/XX/XX.

Type in this access code to attend a
FREE WEBINAR
"100 Tips for More Effective Sales Presentations."
at www.freetips.com.

Equivalent to a $500 live seminar! Just one tip could increase your sales by 10%!

To participate in our Webinar, visit our Web site anytime before 5 PM 9/23/08 at www.freetips.com and type in this access code: GE45Tm72.

Limit: one free Webinar per code. Hurry! offer expires 04/05/09.

Present this coupon for a
free sample of our new perfume.
PHOTO: ROMANTIC SHOT OF MODEL
AND PERFUME BOTTLE WITH PERFUME LOGO

An original fragrance for the adventurous woman from The House of Givenchy.

Redeemable at any participating perfume purveyor. Visit our Web site at www.chainofscents.com for the store nearest you. Limit: one per customer. Void where prohibited by law. Offer expires 08/04/09.

Promotional Offer

As with coupons, the primary purpose of promotional offers is to encourage people to try something immediately. A promotional offer can push customers who are on the bubble to act now. A promotional offer can encourage regular customers to try new products or services, to buy more expensive products or services, or to purchase more frequently.

The great danger of promotions, as with coupons, is that they can become addictive. If you do promotions, sales go up in the short term, but over time promotions can accustom customers to expect deals and discounts. As a result, they wait for promotional offers and expect them and even become resentful if you don't offer a discount. This cheapens the perception of your brand's value. Promotions ultimately favor the companies with the financial resources and the volume to survive for a longer time the lower profits of giving something away.

Make sure your promotions match your brand. For products or services costing over $100, it's usually wiser to discount by a percentage. For products or services costing under $100, it's usually wiser to discount by a cash amount. If you have a prestige or luxury brand, think twice about doing any kind of promotion.

Customers vary in their responses to promotions. Take coupons, for example. As mentioned earlier, there are "professional coupon collectors" who chase the biggest savings and will not become long-term customers, there are people who do not use coupons at all, and there are folks in between, who use coupons occasionally, especially for specific products and services.

The best promotions are unexpected and unusual. Customers appreciate them but don't expect them—or ignore them. And they are true to your brand promise and brand personality. Promotional offers should work with your brand communications to attract new customers or encourage current customers to try more products or services.

A promotional offer can be placed in almost any part of your communication: headline, coupon, body copy, starburst, or outer envelope. Or it can be added as a separate piece that accompanies your main message.

Direct response researchers know that changing the promotional offer from "Buy one, get one free" to "Save 50%" can make a big difference in sales results, even though it has the same financial cost to your company. It pays to constantly test different offers by putting on each offer a special order number or an address, telephone number, or e-mail address specific to that offer.

You're probably familiar with phrases like "Offer expires 4/4/08" or "Void where prohibited by law" or "No purchase necessary to win" or "Limit: one per customer." There are many phrases regarding promotional offers that are required by law, to prevent fraud, or to avoid competitive litigation.

Important: Make sure you consult your lawyer before communicating your offer to the public, particularly regarding any contests or guarantees. Almost any promotional offer should be accompanied by conditions or time limits. The language for these conditions and limits should be supplied by your lawyer.

17 Creative Approaches to Writing a Promotional Offer

1. CREATE A CONTEST

- You may already be a winner!
- Congratulations! You've won at least one of three prizes.
- Scratch and win.
- Visit our Web site, enter the number below, and you may be an instant winner.
- Today's 100th caller wins a shopping cart full of prizes.
- You could win a new home worth $125,000!
- Between now and April 3rd, 20 people will win $1000 each. Will you be one of them?
- It's time once again for our Annual Free-Trip-to-Hawaii Contest.
- The winner gets a one-year supply of gasoline, absolutely free!
- The more you buy, the better your chances to win.
- Free lottery ticket with every $100 purchase.

2. HAVE A SALE

- It's time for our annual Back-to-School Sale.
- Announcing our Christmas-in-July Sale.
- Save as much as 50% at our Grand Opening Sale.
- St. Patrick's Day Clothing Sale. 50% off anything green.
- Don't miss our 24-hour Surprise Sale.
- Seven days of savings during our Weekly Deal Days.
- Hurry—sale ends this Thursday!
- Introducing our 1/10 Sale. Buy one. Save 10%.
- Clearance Sale. Save up to 40%.
- Thank-You Sale. To thank you for your business.

3. OFFER FREEBIES

- Free balloons for the kids!
- Free calculator with every purchase over $50.
- Buy a new car and we'll give you a new 26-inch color TV for free.
- To say thanks for your business, we'd like to give you 10% off your next purchase.
- Buy today and get a free annual subscription to X Magazine worth over $25.
- A $35 value! Buy one and get one free.
- Get a premium car wash and we'll throw in a free air freshener. Your choice of scent.
- Free ice cream when you order a Kid's Meal.
- Upgrade your ticket and enjoy full VIP Club privileges for one day.

4. OFFER SAVINGS

- Get 10% off your next purchase.
- $1.00 off your next purchase.
- Save $10 on every $100 of material you buy.
- To thank you for your business, we'd like to give you a 20% discount on your next purchase.
- Buy 10. Save 10%.
- Why pay full price when you can save $40?
- 15% off the list price.
- Enjoy a 20% discount on any order over $200.

5. FEATURE LOW PRICES

- If you can find it at a lower price, buy it there.
- Competitively priced sofas and recliners.
- Where you enjoy everyday low prices.

- At these prices, you don't need to look for sales.
- Nobody underprices Linoleum World. Nobody.
- Rock-bottom prices. Tip-top values.
- You'll find our services are affordably priced.
- We're not the cheapest, but we're the best value.
- Our policy is to always remain competitively priced.

6. PROVIDE A FREE EVALUATION

- Mail in this form and we'll give you a free painting estimate.
- Answer this brief questionnaire and we'll give you three options and a recommendation at no charge.
- Call XXX-XXXX and we'll send an expert to your home to do a free water quality analysis. There is no obligation to buy.
- Are you paying too much or too little for life insurance? Our free Life Insurance Review can tell you.
- If you answered yes to five or more of these questions, you could be losing up to 30% of your profits to poor personnel practices.

7. OFFER A REBATE OR REFUND

- Buy now and we'll send you a check for $100.
- $400 rebate on purchases of $1000 or more.
- Get a 46% rebate!
- If you decide to purchase our complete training kit, we'll refund your down payment.
- If you're not absolutely satisfied, send the CDs back at our expense and keep the first CD free.
- To thank you for your business, here is a $10 refund check.
- Get a $20 manufacturer's rebate.

8. DONATE TO A GOOD CAUSE

- This month, a portion of your purchase will be donated to Kids Against Cancer.
- 10% of our sales will be given to Seniors Without Partners.
- One dime of every dollar you spend will go to support The March of Dimes.
- Buy a pair of shoes for yourself and we'll donate a pair of shoes to a needy family.

9. MAKE A LIMITED OFFER, TO ENCOURAGE IMMEDIATE ACTION

- Hurry! Supplies are limited.
- The first 100 customers to sign up for gym membership will get a free massage.
- The 50th caller today will win $100.
- Hurry! Offer ends at 5 pm this Saturday, 4/14/07.
- Final Clearance Sale. Everything must go!
- Don't miss the last day of our annual sale or you'll have to wait another 361 days.
- At these prices, these motorcycles won't last long. So come in today.
- Don't wait and miss out. Call now and reserve your seat with a credit card.

10. CREATE A SAVINGS CLUB

- Members receive regular 10% discounts on all products and services.
- Join our Frequent Buyers Club and get the maximum savings.
- If you buy more than five books a year, your Reader's Card will pay for itself.

■ Members of our rewards program get sale notifications and the highest discounts.

11. REWARD SPECIFIC KINDS OF CUSTOMERS

■ Discount prices for seniors with ID or AARP card.

■ Senior discounts.

■ Children under 4 eat free.

■ Student discounts.

■ Group discounts available.

■ Groups of ten or more save 10%.

■ Ladies drink free on Tuesdays.

■ Free birthday cake with driver's license.

12. TURN CUSTOMERS INTO SALESPEOPLE

■ For every customer you sign up, we'll give you $10 off your next purchase.

■ Bring a friend and get a free dessert.

■ Host a sales party and earn $100 worth of free merchandise.

■ Sign up friends and family and you will all save 10%.

13. PROVIDE FREE INFORMATION

■ Send for a free brochure, "How to Grow Bigger Tomatoes."

■ Send for a free home self-test kit.

■ Download "100 Tips for More Effective Sales Presentations" free at www.freetips.com.

■ For a free white paper on "How to Find the Most Powerful Thing to Say to Persuade Your Customers," visit www.barrycallen.com or send an e-mail to barry.callen@gmail.com.

14. REWARD PEOPLE FOR ATTENTION

- Watch this online presentation for ten minutes and we'll mail you a check for $10.
- Sign up to receive our newsletter and get $20 off your next purchase.
- Anyone who attends our home sales party will walk away with a free set of steak knives.
- Win one of three great prizes just for listening to our sale pitch.

15. PROVIDE A SPECIAL EVENT

- Hear automotive expert Bob Udely talk about "Ten Ways to Prevent Expensive Car Repairs."
- Grand Opening. Toys. Games. Prizes. Refreshments. Free!
- Sneak Preview Sale for our Rewards Customers.
- Free wine-tasting party at Oliver's Vinery and Winery.

16. MAKE A GUARANTEE

- If you're not absolutely satisfied, we'll give you a full refund.
- If you can find a lower price, we'll match it.
- Satisfaction guaranteed or your money back.
- If we don't fix it right the first time, we'll fix it free the second time.

17. PROVIDE A FREE SAMPLE

- Send for a free sample of our new perfume.
- Enclosed please find a free sample of our new Maxgrit sandpaper, courtesy of Smithson Industries.
- Download one free song from our band at www.ourband.com.
- Thursday is Free Sample Day at Owens Delicatessen. Stop by and eat up!

Chapter 7
Tactics for Web Site Advertising

People don't go online to be interrupted by advertising or to read information. They go online to quickly find, scan, browse, download, contact, or purchase something that interests them. They like to be able to click through pages as rapidly as possible, with a minimum of interruption or confusion, and they like to retrace their steps quickly if they hit a dead end. The more they have to stop and think about where they are or how to get to where they want to be, the more likely they are to click out of your Web site. In fact, visitors can get downright angry if you try to slow them down.

There are eight parts to a Web site home page:

1. Name
2. Tagline or Summary
3. Category Buttons
4. What's New/Features
5. Promotions
6. Summary of What You Can Do Here

7. Registration Bar/Log-in Bar
8. Search for

Fortunately, there are many conventions for Web sites—words or design elements that most people use in a similar way on their Web sites. For example, a search feature typically involves the word "search" next to a blank box. Visitors to a site know to type a word or a string of words in the box and click the search button. So you can spare your users a lot of frustration if you use conventional wording and design instead of inventing something clever, such as "Go find it now" or "Fetch information." The shorter and clearer and more conventional your words and sentences and paragraphs are, the better.

Web sites have become essential communication sources in many situations. For example, before a reporter writes a story about a company or product and before calling a company representative, he or she almost always goes online and checks out the company or product there first. Many consumers will do the same because they can window-shop many options quickly 24/7 anywhere in the world and avoid a pushy salesperson. In general, the younger and more educated your target market, the more likely your potential customers are to use your Web site.

These elements are most responsible for attracting people to your Web site:

1. Your name: the easier to spell and remember, the better
2. The meta words you include in your Web pages: they may cause search engines to place your site higher in the listings they generate
3. The links you create with related Web sites
4. Your home page

Your home page is like your front door or the front of your store. For the first visit, many people will enter your site through your home page. After that, they may bookmark a particular page on your site and enter through that door instead.

It is usually good to put a button on every page titled "home" that makes it easy to return to your home page from any other page on your Web site.

Creative Tip: Don't try to do everything on your home page or it will become too confusing to use. Make sure you know the most common reasons people use your Web site and organize the information (your Web architecture) around those reasons. Make sure your site designer uses as many design conventions as possible and uses design to provide a clear hierarchy of information.

Creative Tip: Avoid using selling or advertising words. Instead, provide helpful information. Keep all your writing short, sweet, and concrete. People visiting home pages don't read. They scan.

Dos and Don'ts

- Do invest time to include the right meta words that trigger search engines to bring your site up. Start by asking prospective customers what words they would use to find a business or product like yours. You'd be surprised what words they might try—and how they might spell those words.

- Don't try to offer the users a lot of choices. For any section, a good rule of thumb is to give no more than five to eight choices.

- Do use Internet conventions for wording, design, and navigation.

- Do make your site as interactive as possible and as little like a brochure as possible.
- Do continuously update your site so that there is always something new and fresh.
- Do check out your competitors' Web sites. Imitate what works well. But find a way to make your site different and better.
- Don't put design and creativity ahead of functionality. Make your site quick and easy to use.
- Don't make it necessary for your users to stop and think.

Home Page

On the following pages are some suggestions for creating perfect phrases for each section of your home page.

Name

The culture of the Internet allows you to be more creative and "out there" in naming your Web site. Partly, this is because most obvious names are already taken. Partly, this is because the more unusual the name, the easier it is to remember.

To create a better business or product name, use the 23 creative approaches presented in Chapter 2:

- Combination
- Soundalike
- Phrase
- Benefit
- Visual image
- Oxymoron
- Alliteration
- Rhyme

- Foreign
- Place
- Wordplay
- Mythology
- Animals
- Colors
- Personal names
- Letters
- Unrelated borrowing
- Sound effect
- Verbs
- Personification
- Target market
- Slang
- Category label

Tagline or Summary

What does your Web site help people do? Whom does your Web site serve? How is your Web site different from other choices?

If your name does not answer at least one of these three questions, then the line beneath your name should answer one or more of them. If your tagline is too vague, then don't use it. Instead, write a short, sweet, and concrete summary that answers at least one of those three questions. As soon as people land on your home page, they want to know what they can expect there. And they won't wait around to figure it out. So make sure this line is visually prominent and effective.

Use the 23 creative approaches to writing a business tagline, theme line, or slogan (Chapter 2, pages 13–19).

- Ask a question.
- Use alliteration.
- Use rhyme.
- Use rhythm.
- Use an oxymoron.
- Tie it to a name.
- Position with associations.
- Position against competitors.
- Keep it short and conversational.
- Use an analogy, a simile or metaphor, or a symbol.
- Paint a picture.
- Dramatize it.
- Tie it to a physical attribute.
- Include your customers.
- Tie it to a time or a place.
- Express a feeling.
- State a position.
- Call for action.
- State a benefit.
- Use unusual words.
- Make it the voice of a character.
- Play with words.
- Use your category descriptor.

Category Buttons

Category buttons divide your Web site into navigable areas. You can think of your home page as the foyer of your home and the category buttons as doors leading to other rooms: kitchen, bathroom, living room, utility room, basement, and so on. It's important that the sign you put on each door give them a good idea of where it leads. That way, they can quickly find what interests them.

There can be layers upon layers of category buttons as the user goes deeper into your Web site. You want to keep the number of doors small enough for the user to scan quickly and understand and large enough to offer sufficient choices. Five to eight choices is usually ideal.

So, to continue our analogy with your home, once users click on "kitchen," you may want to offer them doors labeled "cupboard," "refrigerator," "sink," "silverware," "plates," "oven," and so forth. And when they click on "plates," you might offer them doors labeled "paper," "fine china," "plastic," and "everyday."

You can think of this layering as a kind of branching, where each thing leads to several others, each of those things, in turn, leading to several others. The number of branches and their order and connections are what is known as the architecture of your Web site.

There are a million ways to branch category buttons, but here are a few words and phrases that are commonly used and therefore easier for users to understand.

Six Creative Approaches to Writing Category Buttons

1. DIVIDE YOUR CATEGORIES INTO DEPARTMENTS

- Engineering, Sales, Installation, Repair, Billing, Customer Service
- Manufacturing, Distribution, Pricing, Promotion, Forecasting, Personnel
- Televisions, Cameras, Stereos, Computers, Printers, Telephones
- Account Management, Creative, Media, New Media, Production, Billing, Public Relations, Research

2. DIVIDE YOUR CATEGORIES INTO ACTIONS

- Browse, Join, Search, Order, Track Order, Contact Us
- Games, Puzzles, Songs. Chat, Blog, Download, E-mail, Report Spam
- Deposit, Withdrawal, Transfer, Check Balance, Create New Account, Research, Contact Banker
- Accounting, Scheduling, Billing, Pharmacy, Web, Patient Records

3. DIVIDE YOUR CATEGORIES INTO LOCATIONS OR GEOGRAPHIC AREAS

- 53702, 53703, 53704, 54987, 54992
- Illinois, Indiana, Iowa, Kentucky, Michigan, Ohio, Wisconsin,
- Northeast, Northwest, Southeast, Southwest, South Central, Central, Mountain
- North America, South America, Europe, Asia, Africa
- USA, France, Germany, Ireland, England, Scotland, Italy

4. DIVIDE YOUR CATEGORIES INTO PEOPLE TYPES

- Collectors, Dealers, Distributors, Interior Designers, Architects, Specifiers, Others
- Painters, Sculptors, Dancers, Actors, Musicians, Donors, Volunteers
- Families, Children, Seniors, Groups, Individuals
- Lesbian, Gay, Bisexual, Transgender, Bisexual, Straight Male, Straight Female, Bicurious
- Publishers, Editors, Writers, Printers, Retailers, Distributors, Resellers
- Lawyers, Police Officers, Social Service, Teachers, Parents, Volunteers

5. DIVIDE YOUR CATEGORIES INTO INTENTIONS OR OCCASIONS

- Fishing, Hunting, Camping, Boating, Hiking, Biking, Swimming
- Birthdays, Anniversaries, Funerals, Christenings, Weddings, Holidays
- Breakfast, Brunch, Lunch, Dinner, After-Dinner, 24/7
- Planning, Tilling, Digging, Fertilizing, Planting, Pruning, Pest Control
- Meeting, Wedding, Convention, Free Events, Hotel, Transportation, Sightseeing

6. BORROW COMMONLY USED CATEGORY BUTTON NAMES (CONVENTIONS) AND MIX AND MATCH

- About Us
- Advertise
- Archives
- Articles
- Blogs
- Browse
- Buy
- Chat Rooms

Tactics for Web Site Advertising

- Checkout
- Company Info
- Contact Us
- Customer Service
- Demo
- Directories
- Directory of Members
- Directory of Services
- Discussion Boards
- Downloads
- Employment
- Favorites
- FAQs
- Forums
- Gallery
- Games
- Gifts
- Help
- History
- Home
- How to Buy
- How to Shop
- Investor Relations
- Jobs
- Join
- Member Login
- Music
- My _____
- News
- Order Tracking

- Photos
- Press Release
- Print
- Privacy Policy
- Products
- Register
- Report Spam
- Reviews
- Search
- Search Site
- Sell
- Service Locator
- Shopping Cart
- Sign In
- Sign Up
- Site Directory
- Site Map
- Speeches
- Store Locator
- Support
- Survey
- Tech Help
- Testimonials
- Top Sellers
- Video
- View Cart
- Welcome
- What's New
- White Papers
- Your Account

What's New/Features: Three Creative Approaches to Writing a What's New/Features Section

1. USE THE 11 CREATIVE APPROACHES TO WRITING A FIRST PARAGRAPH FOR PRINT ADS

(Chapter 3, pages 37–42)

- State the most important thing your company, product, or service will do for customers.
- State why customers should care about the point you make in the headline and subhead.
- State whom your company serves, what you do, and how you are different.
- Open with a surprising fact.
- Open with a promotional offer.
- Challenge one of the customers' assumptions.
- Open with news.
- State why your topic is timely. Answer the question, "Why now?"
- Show you understand the customers' point of view by describing it.
- Acknowledge a difficult truth and then state why customers need not worry about it.
- Summarize your main persuasive arguments.

2. USE THE FOUR CREATIVE APPROACHES TO WRITING BODY COPY FOR PRINT ADS

(Chapter 3, pages 43–44)

- List multiple features, services, and/or benefits.
- Provide reasons to believe your main claim.

- Give an example.
- Use photos/illustrations and captions.

3. USE THE 18 CREATIVE APPROACHES TO WRITING HEADLINES

(Chapter 2, pages 21–27)

- State a tangible benefit involving time, money, safety, or ease.
- State an emotion benefit that fulfills a desire or alleviates a fear.
- State a problem and provide a solution.
- Provide a demonstration.
- Announce news.
- Flag the prospect.
- Ask a question.
- Offer savings.
- Offer freebies.
- List helpful how-tos.
- Tell a story.
- Shock and surprise.
- Use humor.
- Use drama.
- Use an expert endorsement.
- Use a customer testimonial.
- Acknowledge a typical bias, opinion, or problem in the headline and then refute it in the body copy.
- Associate with a good cause.
- Tell a story.
- Shock and surprise.
- Use humor.

- Use drama.
- Use an expert endorsement.
- Use a customer testimonial.
- Acknowledge a typical bias, opinion, or problem in the headline and then refute it in the body copy.
- Associate with a good cause.

Promotions: Use the 17 Creative Approaches to Promotion to Encourage Action

WARNING: Make sure you check with a lawyer before making any promises or guarantees or claims.

- Create a contest.
- Have a sale.
- Offer freebies.
- Offer savings.
- Feature low prices.
- Provide a free evaluation.
- Offer a rebate or refund.
- Donate to a good cause.
- Make a limited offer, to encourage immediate action.
- Create a savings club.
- Reward specific kinds of customers.
- Turn customers into salespeople.
- Provide free information.
- Reward people for attention.
- Provide a special event.
- Make a guarantee.
- Provide a free sample.

Seven Creative Approaches to Writing a Summary of What You Can Do Here

1. USE THE FIVE W'S AND ONE H: WHO, WHAT, WHEN, WHERE, WHY, HOW

- **Who:** Corprov is Improv training for Corporations. The founder and chief instructor is Barry Callen, who has over 14 years of experience as an improv comedian and teacher.

- **What:** Corprov classes consist of improv games that anyone can play. No one has to perform or be funny.

- **Why:** The games teach skills that are useful in the corporate world, such as creativity, presentation, listening, leading, following, thinking on your feet, and teambuilding. It's so much fun that it also builds morale.

- **Where:** All you need is enough space and privacy to jump around and be loud. Corprov can travel to a location of your choosing. Ideal for retreats.

- **When:** The ideal seminar starts at 8:30 a.m. and ends with lunch at 12:30 p.m., but any four-hour period will work. Classes have been held in the morning, afternoon, and evening, weekdays and weekends.

- **How:** One instructor can handle up to 40 participants at a time. All the participants need is comfortable clothing. There are no PowerPoint slides or leave-behinds because they learn by doing. To schedule a class, contact Corprov at 608.347.8396.

2. SUMMARIZE THE LIST OF THINGS THEY CAN DO ON YOUR SITE

Make each thing you list a link (usually underlined and in blue), so users can go right to it if they are interested.

- Corprov is Improv training for Corporations. The founder and chief instructor is Barry Callen, who has over 14 years of experience as an improv comedian and teacher.
- You can use this Web site to:
  __ Check out class dates available
  __ Tentatively hold a date
  __ Book a class
  __ Take a test to see if these classes would help your company
  __ Prioritize and set learning objectives
  __ Search classes by improv game
  __ Review requirements: time, space, money, number of students
  __ Hear testimonials from past participants and corporations
  __ Download a proposal for class to submit for approval
  __ Play online improv games
  __ Contact us for more information

3. USE A WELCOME LETTER FORMAT

Welcome to the Corprov Web site!

Here you will find ways to improve the skills of your team using improvisational comedy games that have been adjusted for use in the corporate and non-profit worlds. Wouldn't you love it if your colleagues were …

- More creative?
- Better listeners?

- Better leaders?
- Better followers?
- More confident presenting?
- Happier and more fun?
- More open to new ideas?
- Better able to think on their feet?

That's why I created these improv classes. As the Creative Director and Managing Partner of an advertising agency, I found that our morale and our creativity were being dulled by the daily grind of business. So I took the games I learned at Second City and simplified them so that anyone can play them. The classes worked so well that we used them for years and our clients began requesting them too.

These classes are also perfect for any retreat or event where your goal is to inspire your employees to think outside the box. Enjoy!

Barry Callen
Founder
Corprov
Corporate Improv

P.S. It's easy to schedule a class or even reserve a date. You can do it in minutes!

4. USE THE 11 CREATIVE APPROACHES TO WRITING A FIRST PARAGRAPH FOR A PRINT AD

(Chapter 3, pages 37–42)

- State the most important thing your company, product, or service will do for customers.

- State why customers should care about the point you make in the headline and subhead.
- State whom your company serves, what you do, and how you are different.
- Open with a surprising fact.
- Open with a promotional offer.
- Challenge one of the customers' assumptions.
- Open with news.
- State why your topic is timely. Answer the question, "Why now?"
- Show you understand the customers' point of view by describing it.
- Acknowledge a difficult truth and then state why customers need not worry about it.
- Summarize your main persuasive arguments.

5. USE THE FOUR CREATIVE APPROACHES TO WRITING BODY COPY FOR PRINT ADS
(Chapter 3, pages 43–44)

- List multiple features, services, and/or benefits.
- Provide reasons to believe your main claim.
- Give an example.
- Use photos/illustrations and captions.

6. USE THE EIGHT CREATIVE APPROACHES ON THE RADIO TO EMOTIONALLY HOOK LISTENERS
(Chapter 4, pages 97–103)

- Tell a story.
- Quote a person.
- Paint a sensory picture that puts the listener in the scene.
- Dramatize the need.

- List customer choices.
- List features and benefits.
- Describe what is unique or unusual or extreme.
- Contrast the experience you provide with a typical customer experience.

7. USE THE 13 WAYS ON THE RADIO TO PROVE THAT LISTENERS CAN BELIEVE YOU
(Chapter 4, pages 104–111)

- Prove customer satisfaction.
- Prove leadership.
- Provide a customer testimonial.
- Provide an expert testimonial.
- List credible endorsements.
- List certifications and memberships.
- Offer a guarantee or make-good.
- Prove quality.
- Offer a compelling or unusual statistic, the more precise the better.
- Invite skeptics to see for themselves.
- State a growth fact.
- List years of experience.
- Prove authentic motivation or passion.

Chapter 8
Tactics for Press Releases

D on't bother doing a press release unless you have genuine news that readers will be interested in. You will only irritate the publication editor by wasting their time. This will reduce your chances of getting news coverage in the future. It is not enough, for example, to announce a new product. Businesses announce new products all the time. If you are announcing the world's first personal computer or a new low-cost cancer cure, you are far more likely to get news coverage.

Examples of genuine news include firsts, bests, awards, surprises, new information, associations with celebrities, or anything that is unusual or out of the norm. "Dog bites man" is not news. "Man bites dog" is. If you have an experience that makes a surprising or entertaining photo or video, such as "eating the world's largest pizza," then you could get newspaper or television coverage.

The exception to this rule is when you hire a new employee or add a new client. Trade publications or the business pages of consumer publications often have sections specifically devoted to these types of announcements. If you can, include your new employee's photograph. Another exception is business special sections that include business directories, such as listings of "The top 100 employers in Wayne County."

In general, a press release should not exceed one or two pages. If you want to include additional information, such as company history, or biographies, or photos, or video, put it just behind the press release (separate, not attached) within the same folder or kit.

Dos and Don'ts

- Don't send out a press release if you do not have genuine and surprising news for readers or viewers. You will damage your chances of getting coverage from that editor in the future.
- Do send out releases when you have genuine news: a first, an only, a surprise, a rarity, or a special event.
- Do announce new hires and new client acquisitions. Be sure to include a photo for new hires.
- Do stick to the format provided. Use the conventions for your press release, such as "contact person."
- Do use the "inverted pyramid" style of writing. Put your most important points first, second-most important points second, and least important points last.
- Do include photographs or DVDs (4 x 5" photos, or better yet, put them on a DVD).
- Do keep your press release short and to the point. Try not to exceed two typed double-spaced pages.
- Don't brag or use excessive adjectives. Instead use facts and quotes and concrete descriptions.

The Six Parts of a Press Release

1. Release Statement

In the upper left hand corner, type the words "FOR IMMEDIATE RELEASE." Make sure you use all capital letters as in this example.

Or, if it is important that your information be released on a certain date, type the words "FOR RELEASE ON XX/XX/XX."

2. Contact Person

Type the contact information two lines below the release statement. Make sure you include the name of the one spokesperson the news media should contact with any questions. Include this person's title, and all the numbers to contact them at any hour of the day or night. Include daytime and evening phones, fax, and e-mail. Reporters are usually on deadline, so they need to reach you right away, day or night, weekday or weekend.

Laura Carroll
Founder, President, CEO
Laura's Chocolate Truffles
Cell Phone: XXX XXX XXXX
Home Phone: XXX XXX XXXX
Office Phone: XXX XXX XXXX ext. XXX
Fax: XXX XXX XXXX
Daytime e-mail: laurac@chocotruffles.com
Evening e-mail: lctruffalicious@gmail.com

3. Headline

This is the single most important part of your release. If there is no news or hook here, editors will read no further.

Type this two spaces below the contact information. Type it using bold lettering, like this.

EXAMPLE: **Introducing the first chocolate truffle that is safe for diabetics**

4. Date and Place

List the date you are releasing the information and the location it is originating from. This is sometimes called the "dateline." EXAMPLE: Milwaukee, Wisconsin 2/10/20__

5. Opening Paragraph

Put your strongest, most provocative, most interesting, most useful, or most surprising information here. Your job is to grab the readers' attention and get them to care enough to read the rest of the article. Most editors will not read beyond this point if your content is not newsworthy enough.

Use the 11 creative approaches to writing body copy for magazine and newspaper ads (see pages 37–42):

- State the most important thing your company, product, or service will do for customers.
- State why they should care about the point you make in the headline and subhead.
- State who your company serves, what you do, and how you are different.
- Open with a surprising fact.
- Challenge one of their assumptions.
- Open with news.
- State why your topic is timely. Answer the question "Why now?"
- Show you understand the person's point of view by describing it.
- Acknowledge a difficult truth, and then state why they need not worry about it.
- Summarize your main persuasive arguments.

6. Main Body or Text

If you have succeeded in grabbing attention and interest in your first paragraph, you can add interesting details or examples here. Be sure to keep your writing as brief as possible. Put your most interesting and newsworthy points first, second-most interesting points second, and so on.

The remainder of the body text should include any information relevant to your products or services. Explain the benefits of your product and why your product or service is unique. Include quotes from celebrities, staff members, industry experts or satisfied customers. (Be sure to get their permission in writing first. Check with your lawyer.) You can also give a brief description of your company or your company history, such as company name, what business you are in, how long you've been in business, and where you are located. Be sure to keep it brief.

Use the four creative approaches to writing body copy for print ads (pages 43–44):

- List multiple features, services, benefits
- Supply reasons to believe your main claim
- Give an example
- Use photos/illustrations and captions

Five Creative Approaches to Writing Press Release Headlines

1. WRITE ABOUT "FIRSTS"

- Ronban's Hardware sponsors first-ever Middletown Days History Fair.
- Doblennapp's county-wide contest for "Never Before Seen Hairstyle."
- Amtrans invents first GPS clothing child locator.
- Veterinary Clinic offers dogs an "Owner Training Class."
- New "Cushion Concrete Laminate" can cushion falls and prevent injuries.

2. WRITE ABOUT EXTREMES: MOST, LEAST, BIGGEST, SMALLEST, FASTEST

- If there is a strong visual (photo opportunity) associated with your headline (such as a 100-foot-long croissant) include a photo or a DVD clip.
- Oberdunnigian's Bakery bakes 100-foot-long croissant for charity.
- Arlene's Decorating makes the Inc. 100 Fastest-Growth List.
- Longest-hair donor will win a year's free hair-styling at Hair Today Salon.
- Myconsultantrocks.com receives largest number of category hits.
- Online Gift Advisor promises your holiday shopping finished in under 15 minutes.

3. TAKE ADVANTAGE OF TIMELY EVENTS

- As diabetes grows, local chocolatier responds with safe truffle.

- Steenbroth's Service Station gives motorists free "Winter Driving Tips."
- Lasertronicam etches the world's smallest holiday card at the molecular level.
- Company throws big Fourth of July Picnic for veterans instead of employees.
- Corprov celebrates Tenth Anniversary with free improv comedy show.

4. ANNOUNCE NEW EMPLOYEES, CLIENTS, OR OFFICES

- These are particularly good for trade publications in your field, for local or regional business publications, or for the business section of your local newspaper.
- Barry Callen founds Corprov, improvisational comedy training for corporations.
- Stergenmeier joins the Omegalpha Corporation as V.P. Personnel.
- Lingonberry promoted to Associate Manager at BigFatHamburger.
- Acme Consultants purchases majority rights to British competitor.
- Orthoughtics Incorporated adds three new Fortune 500 clients.

5. USE THE 18 PROVEN CREATIVE APPROACHES FOR HEADLINES LISTED ON PAGES 21–27

Make sure you avoid sounding like a telemarketer or used car ad.

- State a physical benefit involving time, money, safety, or ease.

- State an emotion benefit that fulfills a desire or avoids a fear.
- State a problem. Provide the solution.
- Provide a demonstration.
- Announce news.
- Flag the prospect.
- Ask a question.
- List helpful how-tos.
- Tell a story.
- Shock and surprise.
- Use humor.
- Use drama.
- Use an expert endorsement (make sure you get written permission).
- Use a customer testimonial (make sure you get written permission).
- State an objection.
- Acknowledge a bias and disprove it.
- Associate with a good cause.

Appendix
Useful Guides to Better
Writing and Marketing

GENERAL TIPS FOR MORE PERSUASIVE WRITING

***The Sir Winston Method: The Five Secrets of Speaking the
Language of Leadership*** by James C. Humes, Quill, 1993

Winston Churchill went from being one of the worst speak-
ers in history, to one of the best, and he kept notes on which
words to use to write great speeches. Hume is a former presi-
dential speechwriter who summarized Churchill's advice in this
slim, easy-to-use book. The principles of persuasive speech
apply to persuasive advertising.

On Writing Well 30th Aniversary Edition by William K. Zinsser,
HarperCollins, 2006

This is the classic guide to writing non-fiction. It helps us
ovecome the urge to use big long words and complex
thoughts and sentences to show how smart we are. The author
offers the antidote to this tempation in this brief and useful
book. The book serves as an example of the advice it offers.

WRITING FOR SPECIFIC ADVERTISING MEDIUMS

This is PR: The Realities of Public Relations, 9th edition, by Doug Newsom, Judy Turk, and Dean Kruckeberg, Wadsworth Publishing, 2006

This classic and comprehensive guide is often used to train entry-level PR professionals in everything from strategy and event marketing to the right use of styles and formats in press releases.

Don't Make Me Think: A Common Sense Approach to Web Usability, 2nd edition, by Steve Krug, New Riders Press, 2005

Krug is a consultant hired to improve the ease and usefulness of Web sites. In a mercifully brief, easy-to-understand, down-to-earth, kind, and humorous style, Krug offers outstanding practical tips and visual examples for all facets of Web design. You don't have to be an expert to use this book.

Radio Advertising: The Authoritative Handbook, 2nd edition, by Pete Schulberg and Bob Schulberg, McGraw-Hill, 1996

This classic by Bob Schulberg has been updated by his son Pete. It contains some useful information on how to write good radio ads, plus a lot of advice on how to buy the best radio times and formats and how to use co-op dollars wisely.

Ogilvy on Advertising by David Ogilvy, Vintage, 1985

Ogilvy was a copywriter and a leading practitioner of multimedia brand advertising based on consumer research. His book provides an entertaining general survey of how to create more effective advertising in different mediums and for different product areas and market situations. Contains lots of pictures and ad examples.

Tested Advertising Methods, 5th edition, by John Caples and Fred E. Hahn, Prentice-Hall; 1998

Direct-mail advertising uses constant comparative testing to provide clear and measurable feedback on which writing sells and which writing doesn't. This book contains the conclusions from thousands of such tests on which offers work best, which mistakes to avoid, and how to write better headlines and coupons. Even though Caples predates the Internet, human nature has changed very little, so his advice remains relevant today.

RESULTS OF ADVERTISING

What Sticks: Why Most Advertising Fails and How to Guarantee Yours Succeeds by Rex Briggs and Greg Stuart, Kaplan Business, 2006

The authors analyzed the results of over $1 billion worth of advertising and concluded that nearly half of all advertising campaigns don't work. They went on to isolate the factors that increase your chances of success. Before you invest in advertising, it is good to know what works, what doesn't, and why. Factors include targeting the right customers and understanding their unspoken emotional motivators.

When Ads Work: New Proof That Advertising Triggers Sales, 2nd Edition by John Philip Jones, M.E. Sharpe, 2006

When bar code scanner purchase data first became available, the information was correlated with exposure to TV advertising for over 140 products in 2,000 households nationwide. Results showed that different advertising produced radically different results. The effective advertising had both a short-term and long-term effect, giving their brands a decided advantage. There are useful and surprising lessons here for any advertiser.

MARKETING AND MESSAGE STRATEGY

Hitting the Sweet Spot: How Consumer Insights Can Inspire Better Marketing and Advertising by Lisa Fortini-Campbell, Copy Workshop, 2001

An ad can be well written and still miss the mark if the underlying strategy is wrong. For example, are you talking to the right people? Are you appealing to the their deepest emotional needs? Fortini-Campbell brings a researcher's mindset to the qualitative search for the most powerful emotional appeal or "sweet spot."

Message Strategy: Seven Simple Questions You Can Use to Find The Most Powerful Thing to Say by Barry Callen, Free E-White Paper, 2007

While the creative director at a national advertising agency, the author invented a simple process for finding the most powerful thing to say to your target market. This process has been refined and proven for over a decade on thousands of ads for over 100 different clients. The process produces a one-page seven-line blueprint to guide the creation of all your advertising. The process makes your message more clear and focused, more emotionally appealing, more important, more believeable, and more action-oriented. For your free download, send an e-mail requesting "E-White Paper #1PP" to barry.callen@gmail.com or visit www.barrycallen.com.

About the Author

Barry Callen is a marketing and advertising consultant, speaker, and teacher who has worked in all marketing communication media, from TV to direct mail to the Internet. He has also worked all sides of the sales communication equation: salesman, presenter, graphic designer, copywriter, creative director, strategist, market researcher, broadcast pro-  ducer, and client. He is the inventor of a system for developing the most powerful possible message strategy—a system that has been used successfully for the last decade. He brings over 30 years of experience with thousands of sales communications for hundreds of clients, ranging from national consumer brands and B2B to software start-up companies and non-profit organizations, including: RJR Nabisco, First Alert, Shell, Famous Footwear, Culligan, Kraft, Fiskars, Thedacare, Epic Systems, United Way, the Health Care Information Management Systems Society, Huffy, Hanes, Zatarain's, and Coca-Cola. Clients have invested millions of media dollars in his creative ideas and writing. In addition to hundreds of industry creative awards, his creative work has won three national Effie Awards for sales effectiveness.

He delivers seminars to rave reviews on all the topics in this book throughout the United States. and at the University of Wisconsin Graduate School of Business for Executive Education. He also teaches improvisational comedy to corporations through Corprov™.

Visit Barry's Web site at **www.barrycallen.com** or contact him via e-mail at **barry.callen@gmail.com** and by phone at **608.347.8396**.

PERFECT PHRASES
for...

MANAGERS

Perfect Phrases for
Managers and Supervisors

Perfect Phrases for Setting
Performance Goals

Perfect Phrases for
Performance Reviews

Perfect Phrases for
Motivating and Rewarding
Employees

Perfect Phrases for
Documenting Employee
Performance Problems

Perfect Phrases for Business
Proposals and Business Plans

Perfect Phrases for
Customer Service

Perfect Phrases for
Executive Presentations

Perfect Phrases for Business
Letters

Perfect Phrases for the
Sales Call

Perfect Phrases for Perfect
Hiring

Perfect Phrases for Building
Strong Teams

Perfect Phrases for Dealing
with Difficult People

YOUR CAREER

Perfect Phrases for the
Perfect Interview

Perfect Phrases for
Resumes

Perfect Phrases for Negotiating
Salary & Job Offers

Perfect Phrases for Cover
Letters